Bridges to Independence

A Guide to Successfully Parenting Teens and Young Adults with Autism into Adulthood

Magen Ross

© **Copyright 2024 - All rights reserved.**

The content contained within this book may not be reproduced, duplicated or transmitted without direct written permission from the author or the publisher.

Under no circumstances will any blame or legal responsibility be held against the publisher, or author, for any damages, reparation, or monetary loss due to the information contained within this book, either directly or indirectly.

Legal Notice:

This book is copyright protected. It is only for personal use. You cannot amend, distribute, sell, use, quote or paraphrase any part, or the content within this book, without the consent of the author or publisher.

Disclaimer Notice:

Please note the information contained within this document is for educational and entertainment purposes only. All effort has been executed to present accurate, up to date, reliable, complete information. No warranties of any kind are declared or implied. Readers acknowledge that the author is not engaged in the rendering of legal, financial, medical or professional advice. The content within this book has been derived from various sources. Please consult a licensed professional before attempting any techniques outlined in this book.

By reading this document, the reader agrees that under no circumstances is the author responsible for any losses, direct or indirect, that are incurred as a result of the use of the information contained within this document, including, but not limited to, errors, omissions, or inaccuracies.

Table of Contents

INTRODUCTION 1

CHAPTER 1: UNDERSTANDING AUTISM IN TEENAGERS 5
  CHARACTERISTICS OF AUTISM DURING TEENAGE YEARS...5
    Social Communication 5
    Sensory Processing 6
    Interests and Focus...7
    Behavioral Challenges 7
  DIFFERENCES BETWEEN CHILDHOOD AND ADOLESCENT AUTISM 8
  COMMON MISCONCEPTIONS ABOUT AUTISTIC TEENS 10
  IMPACT ON FAMILY DYNAMICS 12
    Stress and Anxiety Levels..13
    Shifting Family Roles 13
    Building Support Networks..14
    Sharing Celebrations and Challenges 14
    Guidelines for Supporting Family Relationships 15
  KEY TAKEAWAYS 15

CHAPTER 2: FOSTERING INDEPENDENCE FROM AN EARLY AGE 17
  DAILY LIVING SKILLS TRAINING...17
  BALANCING SUPPORT WITH INDEPENDENCE...19
    Gradual Release of Responsibility 19
    Recognizing Individual Needs...20
    Creating Safe Spaces for Mistakes 20
    Involvement in Decision-Making 20
    Building Self-Confidence...21
    Setting Boundaries and Expectations...21
    Encouraging Social Interactions...21
    Providing Emotional Support..22
    Balancing Independence and Safety 22
    Collaborating With Educators 22
  INCORPORATING CHOICE-MAKING OPPORTUNITIES 23
    Offering Choices in Daily Activities 24
    Personalizing Interests 24
    Participation in Family Decisions...24

    Self-Directed Learning Opportunities 24
  POSITIVE REINFORCEMENT TECHNIQUES 26
    Behavioral Contracts 26
    Celebrating Achievements 27
    Building a Positive Feedback Loop 27
  KEY TAKEAWAYS 28

CHAPTER 3: DEVELOPING SOCIAL SKILLS 31

  ROLE-PLAYING SOCIAL SCENARIOS 31
  USING SOCIAL STORIES FOR UNDERSTANDING CONTEXTS 33
  FACILITATING PEER GROUP ACTIVITIES 36
  ENCOURAGING EMPATHY AND EMOTIONAL AWARENESS 38
  KEY TAKEAWAYS 40

CHAPTER 4: EDUCATIONAL PATHWAYS AND SUPPORT 43

  INDIVIDUALIZED EDUCATION PLANS 43
  TRANSITION PLANNING IN SCHOOLS 46
  SPECIALIZED LEARNING PROGRAMS 48
    Types of Specialized Programs 48
    Benefits of Specialized Learning 49
    Finding the Right Program 49
    Measuring Success 50
  COLLABORATION WITH EDUCATORS AND SUPPORT STAFF 51
  KEY TAKEAWAYS 53

CHAPTER 5: EMPLOYMENT READINESS AND CAREER PLANNING 55

  IDENTIFYING STRENGTHS AND INTERESTS 55
    Assessing Strengths: Using Tools and Observations 55
    Exploring Occupations With the Right Tools 56
    Creating a Profile to Highlight Skills and Interests 57
    Setting Goals Based on Interests 57
    Practical Advice for Parents 58
  JOB COACHING AND MENTORSHIP 58
  WORK EXPERIENCE OPPORTUNITIES 60
  INTERVIEW PREPARATION AND WORKPLACE ACCOMMODATIONS 63
  KEY TAKEAWAYS 65

CHAPTER 6: HEALTH MANAGEMENT AND SELF-CARE 67

  ROUTINE MEDICAL CARE AND CHECKUPS 67
  MENTAL HEALTH RESOURCES 69
  PROMOTING HEALTHY LIFESTYLE HABITS 71
    Establishing a Balanced Diet 72
    Incorporating Regular Physical Activity 72
    Establishing Sleep Hygiene Practices 73

 Fostering Independence in Self-Care *73*
 MANAGING MEDICATIONS AND THERAPIES 74
 KEY TAKEAWAYS 76

CHAPTER 7: NAVIGATING THE LEGAL LANDSCAPE 79

 GUARDIANSHIP AND DECISION-MAKING 79
  Understanding Guardianship Options *79*
  Legal Competence and Rights *80*
  Transitioning Responsibilities *80*
  Resources for Legal Counsel *81*
 DISABILITY BENEFITS AND SERVICES 81
  Overview of Disability Benefits *82*
  Accessing Local Services *82*
  The Role of Advocacy Groups *83*
  Long-Term Planning for Benefits *83*
 LEGAL RIGHTS IN EDUCATION AND EMPLOYMENT 84
  Educational Rights: IDEA and ADA *84*
  Transition Services in Education *85*
  Legal Protections in Employment *86*
  Resolving Disputes *87*
 TRANSITIONING OUT OF PEDIATRIC CARE 88
  Understanding the Transition Process *88*
  Creating Healthcare Plans *89*
  Involvement in Healthcare Decisions *89*
  Resources for Adult Health Care *90*
 KEY TAKEAWAYS 90

CHAPTER 8: BUILDING A SUPPORT NETWORK 93

 FORMING CONNECTIONS WITH ADVOCACY GROUPS 93
  Understanding Available Resources *93*
  Networking With Peers *94*
  Staying Informed on Legislation *95*
  Access to Training Events *95*
 ENGAGING EXTENDED FAMILY MEMBERS 96
 UTILIZING COMMUNITY PROGRAMS 98
  The Value of Social Skills Groups *99*
  Job Readiness Programs: Preparing for Independence *100*
  Getting Involved in Sports and Recreation Activities *101*
  Maximizing Community Resources for a Smooth Transition *101*
 EFFECTIVE COMMUNICATION WITH THE SUPPORT TEAM 102
 KEY TAKEAWAYS 104

CHAPTER 9: FINANCIAL PLANNING FOR THE FUTURE 105

 BUDGETING AND MANAGING PERSONAL FINANCES 105

  Creating a Budget..*106*
  Developing Saving Habits *106*
  Using Personal Finance Apps...*107*
 Savings Plans and Special Needs Trusts...108
  Types of Savings Plans..*108*
  Establishing a Special Needs Trust *109*
  Funding the Trust *109*
  Reviewing and Updating Financial Plans...*110*
 Accessing Financial Aid and Scholarships...111
 Preparing for Independent Living Expenses...113
  Creating a Realistic Spending Plan *114*
  Exploring Affordable Housing Options *115*
  Building an Emergency Fund *115*
 Key Takeaways..116

CHAPTER 10: PROMOTING SELF-ADVOCACY AND RESILIENCE 119

 Teaching Self-Advocacy Skills 119
  Effective Communication Strategies..*120*
  Identifying Personal Needs *120*
  Setting Boundaries *121*
 Building Self-Esteem and Confidence 122
 Handling Setbacks and Challenges 125
 Encouraging Goal-Setting and Persistence 126
 Key Takeaways..129

CHAPTER 11: TECHNOLOGY AND ASSISTIVE TOOLS 131

 Using Apps for Organization and Reminders 131
  Task Management Apps..*131*
  Scheduling Tools...*132*
  Note-Taking Applications *132*
  Reminder Systems *133*
 Assistive Communication Devices 133
 Educational Software and Resources...135
  Interactive Learning Platforms *136*
  Visual Learning Tools..*136*
  Study Aid Applications *137*
  Online Tutoring Services *137*
  Guidelines for Using Educational Software *138*
 Benefits of Telehealth Services 139
 Key Takeaways..141

CHAPTER 12: CREATING A SAFE AND SUPPORTIVE HOME ENVIRONMENT......143

 Adapting the Home Space for Sensory Needs 143
 Establishing Routines and Structure 145

Safety Measures and Emergency Planning 147
Encouraging Participation in Household Chores 148
Key Takeaways 150

CHAPTER 13: CELEBRATING ACHIEVEMENTS AND LOOKING AHEAD 153

Acknowledging Milestones and Achievements 153
    Celebrating Small Wins 154
    Documenting Progress 154
    Involving Peers and Family 155
    Using Visual Reminders 155
    The Impact of Positive Reinforcement 155
Importance of Positive Reinforcement 156
    Effective Reinforcement Strategies 156
    Setting Clear Goals 157
    Encouraging Self-Reflection 157
    Building a Reward System 158
    Creating a Supportive Environment 158
Planning for Continuous Learning 159
    Identifying Areas for Growth 159
    Exploring Learning Opportunities 159
    Creating a Personalized Learning Plan 160
    Encouraging a Lifelong Learning Mindset 160
Keeping an Open Mind About the Future 161
    Fostering a Flexible Attitude 161
    Encouraging Exploration and Curiosity 162
    Setting Broad Future Goals 162
    Building Resilience Through Challenges 163
Key Takeaways 163

CONCLUSION 165

AUTHOR BIO 169

THANK YOU 171

REFERENCES 173

Introduction

As parents and caregivers of autistic teenagers, you face unique challenges and heartwarming moments in raising a child who views the world differently. This journey brings a mix of highs and lows, where every phase involves both worries and triumphs. Watching your child go through their teenage years can be emotionally challenging. You constantly strive to balance offering the proper support and allowing them room to grow independently. As childhood routines shift, new expectations and uncertainties arise, making you wonder about the future.

You are not alone in feeling this way. Every parent worries about their child's future, but these concerns can feel more urgent for parents of autistic teens. Will they be able to form friendships? Can they cope with school or work responsibilities? How will they function when you are not around to support them? These questions often occupy your thoughts, emphasizing how crucial it is to promote independence. Helping your teen develop self-reliance is not just helpful; it is vital for their growth and future success.

Imagine a scenario where your teen confidently decides about their education and friendships and maybe even lands their first job. Independence is not merely an aspiration; it is a vital step toward adulthood. Every parent wishes to see their child succeed and thrive, and this book aims to be your guide on this journey. Every teenager faces challenges during the shift from adolescence to adulthood. Still, for those with autism, the path can be particularly complex. This guide serves as your compass in the often-confusing territory of adolescence, providing you with tools and strategies to support your teen through their unique journey into adulthood.

This book offers practical tips to help autistic teens shift from juvenility to adulthood. It includes clear advice, real-world examples, and expert insights designed to empower your teen. If you are a parent, caregiver, educator, or professional working with autistic teens, this book caters to your needs. It connects home and school, providing comprehensive resources to ensure your teen receives consistent support in every environment.

To help your teen develop into a confident, independent adult, we will cover a range of critical topics throughout this book. We will delve into developing essential social skills, which can be one of the most significant hurdles for autistic teens. Social interactions are a critical component of everyday life, and helping your teen navigate these can significantly enhance their quality of life. We will explore strategies for building and maintaining friendships, understanding social cues, and managing relationships.

Another critical area we will address is education. From selecting the right school environment to pursuing higher education, we will provide detailed guidance on making informed decisions that align with your teen's strengths and interests. Teens develop essential life skills and build relationships in school, not just focus on academics. We will discuss Individualized Education Programs (IEPs), accommodations, and how to advocate effectively for your teen's needs within the educational system.

Employment is another milestone on the road to independence. We will discuss how to prepare your teen for the workforce, from finding suitable job opportunities to understanding workplace norms and expectations. Employment offers financial independence and promotes a sense of accomplishment and self-esteem. We will share tips on job coaching, interview preparation, and creating a supportive work environment.

Legal rights and responsibilities are also crucial aspects of transitioning to adulthood. We will break down complex topics such as guardianship, financial planning, and disability rights, making them accessible and understandable. Knowing your teen's legal rights empowers you to advocate more effectively and ensures they receive the support they are entitled to.

Healthcare management is another vital topic. As your teen grows older, they will need to take more responsibility for their health and well-being. We will cover teaching self-care skills, managing medications, and navigating the healthcare system. Ensuring your teen understands their health needs and can communicate them effectively is a crucial step toward independence.

We will also examine why community involvement is essential. Being part of a community provides a sense of belonging and support. We will discuss ways to engage your teen in community activities, volunteer opportunities, and social groups tailored to their interests and abilities. A solid support network can significantly impact your teen's life.

This book is not just a collection of strategies; it is a roadmap designed to guide you through each stage of your teen's journey to adulthood. Each chapter builds on the previous one, creating a comprehensive framework that addresses the multifaceted aspects of growing up with autism. By the end of this book, I want you to feel equipped and empowered to support your teen in becoming a confident, independent adult.

The transition to adulthood is a significant step filled with challenges and opportunities. You can successfully guide your teen through this journey with empathy, understanding, and practical strategies. I hope this book becomes a trusted resource, offering you valuable tools and heartfelt support every step of the way. We can work together to help your teen unlock their potential and look ahead to a future full of opportunities.

Chapter 1:

Understanding Autism in Teenagers

You sit across from your teenager at the dinner table, noticing how they meticulously organize their food. As you try to start a conversation, they offer a brief response before retreating into their world. You wonder if it is just typical teenage behavior or something more. These small, everyday moments make you pause and reflect on your teen's challenges. Parenting an autistic teenager brings its own set of joys and hurdles, but knowing what to expect helps. Let us talk about some key characteristics of autism during the teenage years that might be familiar.

Characteristics of Autism During Teenage Years

Understanding teen autism is essential for parents, educators, and caregivers who want to support their development in the best way possible. This section identifies vital attributes and behaviors of autistic teens, including social communication challenges, sensory sensitivities, interests and focus, and behavioral difficulties.

Social Communication

Autistic teens often find social communication challenging, especially when interpreting social cues. They may struggle to read nonverbal signals like facial expressions or body language, leading to peer misunderstandings. These difficulties can make social situations stressful, hindering their ability to build and keep friendships.

Autistic teenagers often interpret sarcasm, irony, and other subtle communication literally, which can create confusion and result in awkward situations or social isolation. For instance, if someone jokingly says, "Nice job," when something has gone wrong, an autistic teen may not pick up on the sarcastic tone and feel confused by the response. Research highlights how sensory processing issues can further complicate these social interactions, making it even harder for teens to feel comfortable with peers (Kojovic et al., 2019).

Verbal communication differences also impact autistic teens. They may speak in a way that seems blunt or too direct, which others might find inappropriate. This can create friction in social situations. You can help by giving clear guidance on social cues and using structured social skills training, such as role-playing and direct instruction, to teach appropriate responses in different scenarios.

Sensory Processing

autistic teens often experience heightened sensitivity to sensory input. They may be susceptible to sounds, lights, textures, or tastes. Noisy or chaotic environments, such as school cafeterias or busy malls, can trigger anxiety or sensory overload, making it difficult for them to concentrate or interact with others.

Research also found that altered sensory processing plays a significant role in how individuals with autism navigate social and adaptive functioning (Kojovic et al., 2019). For some teens, this may result in seeking out specific sensory experiences, like fidgeting or repeating certain activities. For others, it could mean avoiding sensory stimuli, such as covering their ears to block out loud noises or refusing to wear certain fabrics due to their texture.

Effectively managing sensory sensitivities relies on creating a sensory-friendly environment. Providing a quiet space for your teen to retreat when overwhelmed or offering noise-canceling headphones can significantly alleviate stress. It is essential to discuss sensory preferences with your teen and collaborate on effective coping strategies that suit their needs.

Interests and Focus

Autistic teens often show intense focus on specific interests, which can both be a strength and a challenge. These special interests offer comfort and competence, immersing teens in meaningful activities. For instance, a teen fascinated by computers might spend hours learning programming or gaming, which can give them a sense of accomplishment.

Focusing intensely on specific interests can sometimes limit a teen's exposure to new experiences. Although these interests might help them connect with others through related clubs, they can also lead to isolation if they consume too much of their time and energy. Encouraging your teen to explore various activities can help them build a diverse skill set and reduce feelings of isolation.

It is crucial to balance these interests with other responsibilities. Creating a structured schedule allows you to manage time effectively and encourages exploration beyond your comfort zone. Incorporate these interests into your students' education to make learning more engaging and meaningful.

Behavioral Challenges

As autistic teens seek greater independence, behavioral challenges often increase. Resistance to authority or difficulty adjusting to new expectations is common during adolescence, as teens strive to assert their autonomy while still figuring out how to navigate their environment.

Grasping the underlying causes of these behaviors enables you to manage them more effectively. By ensuring clear communication and maintaining predictable routines, you can provide the stability autistic teens need. Involving your teen in decisions about daily activities or schoolwork helps them feel more in control and can reduce resistance.

Explaining the reasons behind rules and expectations can be very helpful. Use visual aids or social stories to clarify why specific behaviors are essential, leading to better understanding and cooperation. Celebrate small achievements and provide positive reinforcement to motivate your teen to maintain desired behaviors.

As you face these challenges with your teen, remember that patience and consistency will significantly support them and help them feel understood.

Now that you have a clearer picture of what autism can look like during the teenage years, let us take a closer look at how it compares to autism in childhood. Understanding these differences can provide valuable insight into how your approach may need to shift as your child grows.

Differences Between Childhood and Adolescent Autism

During adolescence, autistic traits often shift and evolve from childhood patterns, making it crucial for you to grasp these changes to support your teen effectively. One key area of change is emotional regulation. While childhood emotional responses are usually predictable, adolescence can bring less predictable and more intense reactions. Hormonal changes during puberty can amplify existing emotional challenges or introduce new ones. Your teen might struggle to identify or express emotions accurately and feel overwhelmed without understanding the cause. To help monitor emotional triggers use tools like emotion diaries or mood-tracking apps. Additionally, therapy, mindfulness exercises, and deep breathing techniques can aid in managing emotional outbursts more constructively.

Social relationships undergo significant changes during adolescence. Friendships that once focused on shared activities now require deeper emotional connections and more advanced social skills, creating challenges for autistic teens. Challenges with understanding social cues and communication subtleties can make this transition more difficult. To support your teen, encourage participation in interest-based clubs or groups where they can meet peers with similar passions. Schools and community centers can organize structured social activities, allowing teens to interact under guided conditions. This approach creates a supportive environment, easing the shift to more complex relationships.

As teens move through middle and high school, their academic responsibilities grow substantially. The growing demands for organization, time management, and self-advocacy can either provide valuable life skills or become overwhelming for autistic teens. Help your teen manage these challenges using planners or digital calendars to keep track of assignments and deadlines. Teach them to advocate for themselves by clearly expressing their needs and asking for help when needed. Schools and programs focusing on building executive functioning skills can provide the necessary tools to handle academic pressures, helping your teen navigate this stage more effectively.

Adolescence is a crucial time for self-discovery. Autistic teens actively explore their identity during this period. This stage can be empowering yet challenging as they evaluate how autism impacts their abilities, relationships, and future goals. Open discussions about identity, whether within the family or through professional counseling, can guide your teen in understanding these experiences. Peer-led support groups offer a valuable platform for sharing stories and strategies with others who relate to their unique experiences. These conversations can build a positive self-image by highlighting their strengths and addressing their challenges, boosting your teen's confidence in their identity.

Another notable characteristic during this time is the intense focus on specific interests, which can become even more pronounced during adolescence. While these passions can provide comfort and mastery, they may also limit your teen's social experiences if not balanced with other activities. It is essential to guide your teen toward exploring new hobbies or interests, gently encouraging them to step outside their comfort zone while building on their strengths.

During the teenage years, your teen may display behavioral challenges as they seek greater independence. While this challenge is typical of adolescence, it becomes more intricate for autistic teens. Recognize that these behaviors come from a desire for autonomy rather than outright defiance. Establishing consistent yet flexible boundaries allows your teen to feel secure while giving them a sense of independence. By providing choices within these limits, you help them feel more in control, which can reduce resistance and promote cooperation. Positive reinforcement for responsible behavior and clear communication about expectations are essential in managing these challenges effectively.

As your teen grows, these characteristics will continue to evolve, making it essential to stay tuned into their needs and be proactive in providing support.

Next, let us tackle some of the common misconceptions surrounding autistic teens. There is a lot of misinformation that can create unnecessary challenges for both you and your teen. Understanding these misconceptions and their truth can empower you to better advocate for your child's needs.

Common Misconceptions About Autistic Teens

When talking about autism in teenagers, it is essential to challenge the myths and stereotypes that distort our understanding. Labels like "high functioning" and "low functioning" often oversimplify the diverse range of abilities and challenges that autistic teens experience. These terms create a misleading binary view and fail to capture each individual's strengths and needs. For example, a teen might excel in math but struggle with social interactions or daily tasks. By reducing them to simplistic categories, we risk missing opportunities for growth and neglecting areas where they may need support or have the potential to thrive. It is crucial to recognize each autistic teen as an individual rather than fitting them into predefined labels.

A common myth is that autistic teens prefer to be alone and lack interest in making friends. In reality, many autistic teens desire friendships and meaningful connections. Still, they may struggle with the skills needed to form them. Dr. Keefer, an American clinical psychologist, notes that these teens often want to be accepted and share their interests with others (Sarris, 2013). Special interests like video games can help bridge the gap by connecting them with peers with similar passions. Supporting these interests promotes social interaction and encourages emotional growth, assisting autistic teens in building connections while pursuing what they love.

There is also a misconception that autistic teens cannot become independent or make decisions for themselves. In reality, fostering independence is essential. Allowing them to make decisions, whether deciding what to wear or planning part of their daily schedule, boosts their confidence and encourages self-reliance. For instance, by allowing your teen to manage responsibilities like setting a homework routine or organizing their room, you help them build critical life skills that will serve them well into adulthood. With the proper support, autistic teenagers can learn to navigate tasks and decisions independently, just like their peers.

Another common myth revolves around perceptions of intelligence. There is a misconception that individuals with autism are either savants with extraordinary abilities or that they have intellectual disabilities. Both assumptions are inaccurate. Autism does not dictate a specific intelligence level—many people with autism have average or even above-average intelligence. However, traditional measures of intelligence, like IQ tests, often fall short when it comes to evaluating individuals with autism, especially if they face communication challenges. That is why it is crucial to recognize and nurture their cognitive strengths in ways that go beyond conventional testing. For example, an autistic teen might excel at solving complex puzzles or coding but struggle with verbal communication. Understanding and supporting their unique abilities opens up more opportunities for success and growth.

Challenging these myths fosters a more inclusive understanding of autistic teenagers. Parents and caregivers should listen actively to the perspectives of individuals with autism and their supporters. Keeping communication open and consistent helps clarify expectations and rules, making autistic teens feel valued and involved in decision-making. This approach builds trust and creates a supportive environment at home and school.

A deeper understanding of meltdowns and shutdowns is also vital. Autistic teens often experience heightened emotional responses, which can manifest as meltdowns (outward expressions of distress) or shutdowns (inward withdrawal). Identifying triggers, whether it is sensory overload, social stress, or sudden changes in routine, helps caregivers develop coping strategies. For instance, creating a quiet, sensory-friendly space in the home can offer your teen a haven during overwhelming moments. Visual aids and consistent routines are also practical tools to reduce anxiety and provide a sense of control.

Research supports the importance of these strategies. According to the National Institute of Mental Health, consistent routines and visual supports improve daily functioning for many individuals with autism (*Autism Spectrum Disorder*, n.d.). Additionally, autistic teens who had access to structured social opportunities, like clubs or gaming groups, reported higher levels of well-being. These insights remind us that with the correct understanding and support, autistic teenagers can thrive in their social and personal lives.

As you continue supporting your teenager, it is essential to dispel these misconceptions and replace them with informed, compassionate approaches that meet their needs.

Now, let us examine how these realities impact family dynamics and how you can create a balanced, supportive environment for everyone involved.

Impact on Family Dynamics

Raising an autistic teenager can profoundly impact family relationships, often introducing challenges that affect stress levels, family roles, support systems, and the way families share both joys and struggles.

Stress and Anxiety Levels

Caring for an autistic teenager brings distinct challenges that often result in increased stress and anxiety for caregivers. Parents, particularly mothers, usually bear the brunt of this pressure. Many parents experience substantial burnout from the relentless demands of caregiving. Caregivers frequently feel exhausted and overwhelmed, facing emotional and physical fatigue. These feelings are typical among parents balancing work, household duties, and the needs of their autistic teenager.

Burnout is not just a buzzword; it is an honest and exhausting experience that can disrupt the entire family. In this context, prioritizing self-care becomes essential. Regular breaks, setting aside time for personal hobbies, and seeking professional counseling can offer significant relief. Open communication is crucial for the family. It helps everyone stay connected and address issues effectively. Openly discussing stress levels and individual needs fosters empathy and ensures everyone's well-being is prioritized. Promoting understanding can build a supportive family environment where everyone feels valued and cared for.

Shifting Family Roles

Autism can shift the roles within a family, often placing new expectations on siblings. Brothers and sisters of autistic teens may find themselves stepping into caregiver roles, which can sometimes cause feelings of resentment or neglect. For example, one mother, Sofia, shared her guilt about how much time and energy she had to dedicate to her child with autism, leaving her feeling like she was not paying enough attention to her other child. This imbalance can strain sibling relationships.

To address these challenges, prioritize recognizing each child's needs and feelings. Carving out individual time for each one can have a significant impact. This dedicated time lets them express their experiences and ensures they do not feel overlooked. Promote open conversations so siblings can openly express their emotions, fostering a safe environment where they feel valued and understood. Educate siblings about autism to build empathy and a deeper connection, helping them better grasp the behaviors and challenges of their sibling with autism.

Building Support Networks

Building a solid support network is essential when raising an autistic teenager. Managing everything alone can increase stress and feelings of isolation. Families with solid support systems experience lower stress and better quality of life. Engage with local support groups, connect with other parents, and participate in online forums to gain valuable emotional support and practical advice.

Support networks can take many forms. They might include extended family members like grandparents, friends at your place of worship, or autism advocacy groups. Finding people who understand your challenges and can share experiences or strategies can make a significant difference. You can exchange tips on therapists, educational tools, and respite care options that can relieve some pressure from primary caregivers. These networks become a lifeline, allowing you to share your journey with others who truly get it.

Sharing Celebrations and Challenges

While caring for an autistic teenager often involves managing challenges, it is essential not to overlook the small victories. Even small moments can uplift the entire family. Whether it is a breakthrough in communication or your teen successfully navigating a social interaction, celebrating these achievements can bring positivity to your household.

At the same time, tackling challenges together is crucial. Families that recognize and openly discuss setbacks foster an atmosphere of transparency and mutual support. Families who openly share their successes and struggles build stronger emotional bonds and create a more positive home environment.

To help strengthen these bonds, consider establishing family rituals, like weekly game nights or outings. These activities do not just provide entertainment; they reinforce your family's connection and allow every member to feel included and valued. Positive memories from shared activities can reduce stress and help everyone feel a sense of belonging.

Guidelines for Supporting Family Relationships

Fostering an environment that supports healthy family dynamics requires intentional effort. Encourage open discussions about feelings, ensuring every family member has a space to share their thoughts without fear of judgment. Caring for an autistic teen requires emotional effort and every family member shares that responsibility.

Empowering your autistic teenager with self-advocacy skills can also help. Teaching them to communicate their needs and seek help when necessary will foster independence and ease some pressure on the family. As your teen builds these skills, they will become more capable of handling their challenges, easing the emotional burden on parents and siblings.

Remember, no family is flawless, and seeking help when necessary is acceptable. Turn to your support network, consult professionals, or take time to recharge. Prioritizing your well-being is crucial for effectively supporting your teenager. Doing so fosters a resilient, connected family environment where everyone can flourish.

Key Takeaways

- Autistic teens often struggle with social communication, including reading social cues and understanding subtle forms of communication like sarcasm.

- Behavioral challenges may arise as autistic teens seek independence. They often require clear communication and predictable routines to manage effectively.

- Autistic teens begin to explore their identity, which may require open discussions and peer support to foster a positive self-image.

- Autistic teens can develop independence with the proper support and learn decision-making skills through small responsibilities.

Fostering independence becomes more important than ever as your teen grows. Building these skills early sets the foundation for their confidence and self-reliance. Let us look at practical ways to encourage independence from a young age, helping them navigate life with greater ease and self-assurance.

Chapter 2:

Fostering Independence From an Early Age

You watch your teen struggle with a shoelace, determined to tie it without help. You resist the urge to step in, knowing that independence comes from practice. After a few attempts and a sigh of frustration, they finally get it. "I did it!" they exclaim with pride, and you realize that letting them try—however difficult it was to watch—was worth it. Independence does not come all at once but in small victories like this one. You are on the right track.

Now, it is time to take the next step: teaching daily living skills to help them thrive beyond these small moments of success.

Daily Living Skills Training

Providing parents with practical techniques to teach daily living skills can significantly impact fostering independence in your autistic teen. One key area to focus on is basic cooking skills. By teaching your teenager how to prepare simple meals, you are ensuring that they can take care of their own nutritional needs and helping them develop essential fine motor skills and strengthen their executive functioning. Start by introducing easy recipes—something as simple as making a sandwich or assembling a salad is a great place to begin. These tasks allow your teen to practice measuring ingredients, following directions, and using kitchen tools safely. Over time, as their confidence grows, you can move on to more complex dishes, encouraging them to plan meals and understand the steps involved in cooking from start to finish. Every recipe they complete transforms the kitchen into a learning space where they gain valuable life skills while feeling accomplished.

Personal hygiene routines are vital when encouraging independence. For autistic teens, tasks like brushing teeth, showering, or grooming can feel overwhelming. Creating a clear, step-by-step guide for each activity helps make them more manageable. Breaking the tasks into smaller steps reduces intimidation and makes learning more manageable for your teen. Visual schedules or checklists effectively reinforce these routines, giving your teen a structured outline of what to do. The goal is for these habits to become second nature over time. Maintaining good hygiene is vital for their health and self-esteem, and celebrating small achievements helps keep them motivated. A positive and encouraging approach will help your teen feel accomplished as they work toward greater self-reliance in personal care.

Equally crucial in developing independence are household responsibilities. Getting your teen involved in age-appropriate chores can be an excellent way to build a sense of contribution and capability. Start by assigning tasks that match their skill level, such as making their bed, sorting laundry, or setting the table. These everyday responsibilities provide opportunities to learn essential life skills and introduce important concepts like time management and organization. Creating a chore chart or visual schedule can help track these tasks and give your teen a sense of ownership over their duties. Letting them have some input on which chores they would like to take on can further nurture their independence, as it fosters a sense of autonomy and accountability. Over time, these responsibilities become part of their routine, instilling pride in their contributions to the household. By gradually increasing the difficulty of the tasks as they grow more comfortable, you are preparing them for the adult responsibilities they will eventually take on.

Teaching your autistic teen transportation skills is essential for fostering independence. Start by helping them navigate familiar areas like your neighborhood or local community. Show them how to read maps, follow bus or train schedules, and use navigation apps to plan routes.

Practice role-playing scenarios, such as finding the right bus stop or asking for directions. Gradually build these skills to boost their confidence in moving around independently. Be sure to teach road safety rules, including pedestrian signals and street crossing. Begin with short trips and slowly increase the intricacy as they become more relaxed. Mastering public transportation or walking to nearby locations will empower your teen to explore their surroundings confidently and independently.

As your teen's abilities grow, you might find it is a balancing act between offering support and allowing them the space to become more independent. While it is natural to want to step in and help at every opportunity, fostering independence requires giving them the room to try things on their own, even if that means letting them face small challenges or failures along the way. With practice, encouragement, and the right strategies, your teen can thrive in their journey toward independence.

Next, let us discuss how to balance offering support and promoting independence—an essential step in helping your teen navigate life with growing confidence.

Balancing Support With Independence

Finding the right balance between providing help and promoting independence for autistic teenagers is vital in helping them grow into self-reliant adults. This delicate process involves teaching them to make decisions while making sure they feel supported along the way.

Gradual Release of Responsibility

Teaching your teen to ride a bike requires a gradual approach. You would not remove the training wheels and expect them to ride confidently immediately. Instead, you would guide them step by step as they improve their balance and confidence. Fostering independence works the same way. Begin with small tasks suited to their current abilities. For instance, let them choose their outfit for the day and then progress to more complex tasks, like managing a small budget for their belongings. Gradually increasing responsibility helps them build confidence and develop decision-making skills over time.

Recognizing Individual Needs

Each autistic teenager has distinct strengths, challenges, and learning styles, so it is essential to understand these differences. Adapting your methods to fit their needs allows them to progress more effectively. For example, using charts or schedules simplifies task learning if your teen learns visually. Celebrate each accomplishment, regardless of size, to reinforce their skills and build their confidence. Personalizing your approach demonstrates respect for their journey, making their learning experience meaningful and effective.

Creating Safe Spaces for Mistakes

Making mistakes is part of learning; creating an environment where your teen feels safe to fail is essential for their growth. Instead of jumping in with corrections when they make an error, give them space to think about what went wrong and why. This encourages problem-solving and resilience. For example, if they forget to complete a homework assignment, guide them to think about steps to prevent it from happening again rather than simply scolding them. Treating setbacks as learning opportunities helps build their adaptive skills, turning mistakes into valuable learning moments.

Involvement in Decision-Making

When autistic teenagers participate in decisions about their lives, they gain essential benefits. Engaging them in family discussions about daily routines, weekend plans, or vacations helps strengthen their self-advocacy and critical thinking. Involving them helps build a sense of power and responsibility. For example, let them help plan weekly meals by choosing recipes, making a shopping list, and assisting with cooking.

These activities build practical life skills while improving their decision-making and commitment to their choices.

Building Self-Confidence

Independence and self-confidence grow together. When you assign your teen age-appropriate responsibilities, show them you trust their abilities. Begin with easy tasks they can accomplish quickly, like setting the table or feeding a pet, then gradually increase the difficulty as they become more capable. Each completed task boosts their self-esteem. Offer consistent praise for their efforts, focusing on how they approach the task rather than just the result. This feedback boosts their confidence and motivates them to embrace new challenges.

Setting Boundaries and Expectations

Promoting independence requires setting clear boundaries and expectations. A structured environment gives your teen a safe space to practice autonomy without feeling overwhelmed. Maintain a consistent routine for daily activities like waking up, mealtimes, and bedtime. Clearly explain these routines to ensure they understand the importance of time management and staying organized. Establish acceptable behavior rules and ensure they know the consequences of breaking them. For example, you can hold a family meeting to assign chores, create a chore schedule, and agree on task completion rewards.

Encouraging Social Interactions

Developing independence involves more than personal tasks; it also includes mastering social situations. Encourage your teen to join clubs, participate in team sports, or attend social gatherings to build communication and interpersonal skills. Practice social scenarios at home to prepare your teen for real-life interactions. Talk about crucial topics such as making friends, handling peer pressure, and recognizing social cues. By providing guidance, you can boost their confidence in social settings, reduce anxiety, and support their growing independence.

Providing Emotional Support

Helping your teen move toward independence can be stressful for both of you. Maintain open communication by regularly asking your teen about their thoughts and feelings. Listen attentively and empathetically, acknowledging their emotions without immediately offering solutions. Encourage your teen to voice their concerns and express themselves. Your support provides a safety net, giving them the confidence to explore independence without feeling abandoned.

Balancing Independence and Safety

Balancing independence and safety is crucial. Teach your teen key personal safety measures for both online and offline environments. Discuss stranger danger, promote safe internet practices, and prepare them for handling emergencies. Provide basic first aid training and ensure they know essential phone numbers. Talking about risks and safe decisions equips them with the tools to stay safe as they become more independent.

Collaborating With Educators

Schools significantly influence your teen's development. Collaborating with teachers strengthens the strategies you are using at home. Share details about your teen's specific needs and learning style, and keep track of their progress. Attending parent-teacher meetings and staying involved in their education creates a unified support system that consistently nurtures your teen's independence skills at home and school.

As you continue this journey, one key area to focus on is creating opportunities for your teen to make choices.

Incorporating Choice-Making Opportunities

Allowing autistic teens to make decisions is crucial for fostering independence and boosting their self-confidence. Giving them opportunities to make choices empowers them to take responsibility and sharpen essential decision-making skills. In this section, you will find strategies to guide your teen toward becoming more self-reliant.

Encouraging independence starts by giving your teen choices in daily activities. Letting them decide what to wear or eat for breakfast increases their sense of control and eases anxiety. They practice weighing options and considering outcomes through these decisions. For example, choosing a weekend activity makes them feel responsible and proud of the results. Giving choices reduces overwhelm and fosters a calm, supportive environment for learning.

Tapping into your teen's interests is another great way to motivate them. When you encourage them to choose hobbies or activities based on their preferences, they can explore new skills and discover strengths. Whether it is sports, learning an instrument, or a craft, having a say in their extracurriculars can ignite passion and build commitment. For example, suppose your teen shows interest in a robotics club due to a love for technology. In that case, they are more likely to try to improve, which leads to valuable skill development and personal growth. You can support this by offering various options and discussing the potential benefits of each activity.

Involving your teen in family decisions is also a fantastic way to nurture autonomy. Including them in conversations about family matters teaches them to voice their opinions while developing negotiation skills. For instance, inviting your teen to help plan a family vacation or decide on a new family pet allows them to share their thoughts and consider others' needs. This approach boosts their confidence in expressing themselves and makes them feel valued in family decisions.

Self-directed learning plays an essential role in preparing your teen for adulthood. Encouraging them to explore subjects or skills independently can spark personal growth and a passion for learning. For example, if your teen is interested in coding, provide them with online courses or books to guide them in setting their learning goals. This helps them develop valuable skills for their future career while building a sense of accomplishment and readiness for adulthood.

Here are a few strategies to help you apply these ideas:

Offering Choices in Daily Activities

Begin with straightforward decisions and introduce more complex ones as your teen gains confidence. Provide clear options and explain the pros and cons of each. Help your teen think about the outcomes of their decisions so they can learn from the experience.

Personalizing Interests

Present different hobby options and let your teen try out various activities. Support them by offering resources such as classes or clubs. Celebrate their achievements to help them stay motivated and involved.

Participation in Family Decisions

Involve your teen in family discussions appropriate for their age. Ensure their input is respected, even if the final decision does not always align with their preferences. Use family meetings to practice negotiation and compromise.

Self-Directed Learning Opportunities

Encourage your teen to find interesting topics and set specific learning goals. Give them access to helpful resources like books or online courses. Check in regularly to monitor their progress and guide them as needed.

Following these guidelines can create a supportive environment where your teen feels empowered to make choices and learn from their experiences. Striking the right balance between giving freedom and setting boundaries ensures their safety and well-being while increasing their independence, helping build confidence, and preparing them for adulthood.

Making mistakes is a normal part of the learning process, and allowing your teen to experience them is crucial. Decision-making can be challenging, and expecting them always to make the right choice is unrealistic. Making mistakes during adolescence helps your teen build resilience and improve problem-solving skills. When they experience the results of their choices, they gain important insights. Respond calmly and offer guidance as a parent or caregiver, helping them make better decisions without feeling judged.

Creating a learning environment that embraces mistakes as a natural part of growth is essential. Discuss potential risks with your teen and encourage them to consider the outcomes. For instance, if they choose a challenging school project, share your concerns about time management, but allow them to proceed. If things do not go as planned, review what went wrong together and explore ways to improve next time.

Open communication is also crucial. Keeping the lines of communication open helps your teen feel comfortable seeking advice and sharing their thoughts. Regular conversations about their choices and outcomes allow you to discuss important topics like values and long-term goals. You can also model good decision-making by sharing your thought processes, giving your teen a framework for making informed choices.

Now that we have covered how to foster independence, let us focus on encouraging positive behaviors and decision-making using reinforcement techniques.

Positive Reinforcement Techniques

To effectively reinforce positive behavior, identify what genuinely motivates your autistic teen. You can discover these motivators by paying attention to their preferences and interests. Some teens may find activities like video games or hobbies rewarding. In contrast, others might respond better to tangible rewards such as tokens, treats, or stickers. Make sure the rewards are meaningful and genuinely appeal to them.

For example, if your teen enjoys drawing, you can reward them with extra drawing time after completing homework or helping with chores. Linking positive behaviors to meaningful rewards keeps them motivated to learn new skills. The link between effort and reward fosters a sense of achievement and encourages continued involvement. Tailoring reinforcement to their interests effectively promotes growth and skill development.

Behavioral Contracts

A behavioral contract is a great way to encourage self-reliance and teach your autistic teen negotiation skills. It is a written agreement in which you and your teen set clear expectations and rewards. This approach is most effective when you agree on the expectations and rewards.

Start by discussing the behaviors you want to encourage and what rewards your teen finds motivating. For instance, completing all weekly school assignments on time might earn an extra hour of screen time over the weekend. This gives your teen clear guidelines and sets up rewards they care about. Ensure these contracts are achievable and straightforward so your teen feels they can succeed.

Behavioral contracts encourage open communication and negotiation—essential skills for adulthood. By involving your teen in decision-making, you help them gain control and responsibility over their actions. This allows them to understand that their efforts have direct consequences, promoting accountability.

These contracts also create opportunities for family discussions. Your teen learns that their input matters, building trust and helping them feel more confident about taking on responsibilities.

Celebrating Achievements

Celebrating your teen's achievements boosts their confidence. Recognizing their efforts, even in small ways, shows you value their hard work. You do not need grand gestures for celebrations—simple actions like giving verbal praise, offering a high-five, or enjoying a favorite activity together can make a big difference.

For example, when your teen completes a difficult task, highlight their achievement. Commend their hard work and persistence to reinforce the value of their efforts, making it more likely they will want to keep trying. Celebrating with a fun outing or favorite activity strengthens your bond and creates positive memories, reinforcing good behavior.

By consistently recognizing their accomplishments, you help build your teen's self-esteem. Over time, they will see that their effort leads to success, a valuable lesson for living independently.

Building a Positive Feedback Loop

A positive feedback loop works by consistently rewarding your teen's efforts and encouraging them to reflect on their progress. This method reshapes behavior and motivates your teen to take the initiative. When they recognize that their hard work brings positive results, they are likelier to repeat those actions.

When your teen finishes a task without a reminder, recognize it immediately and express appreciation for their initiative. Providing this immediate feedback strengthens the link between their effort and the reward. This boosts their motivation to begin tasks independently, maintaining their self-reliance.

Along with reinforcement, provide time for your teen to reflect. After reaching a milestone, discuss what worked and what could be better. Help them evaluate their strategies and feelings about their progress. This reflection deepens their understanding of success and fosters a growth mindset. When they recognize their strengths and areas for improvement, they take charge of their development.

You can gradually reduce rewards as your teen's behaviors become more consistent. By slowly fading external reinforcement, you help them develop intrinsic motivation—where the satisfaction of completing a task or mastering a skill becomes a reward. They will understand that doing something well feels good, and even more motivating than external rewards.

Your teen will gain the tools to thrive independently through consistent reinforcement, celebrating achievements, and reflection.

Key Takeaways

- Allow teens to practice tasks independently to build confidence and autonomy.

- Balancing support and independence is critical to fostering self-reliance.

- Setting boundaries and clear expectations creates a structured environment for independence.

- Self-directed learning encourages growth and a love for learning.

- Creating a positive feedback loop encourages self-initiative and consistency in behavior.

As your teen becomes more independent, the next step is helping them navigate social interactions. Building meaningful connections and understanding social cues are crucial skills for their growth. In the following chapter, you will learn practical strategies to guide your teen in developing the social skills they need to thrive.

Chapter 3:

Developing Social Skills

You watch your teen struggle to keep a conversation going with a classmate. You are cheering them on, but their blunt responses make you smile. "No, I do not like video games," they say, leaving the other kid unsure what to say next. This is familiar—social interactions seem like a tricky puzzle to them. Remind yourself that learning social skills is necessary because they are not innate. You are not just guiding them; you are learning with them and helping them decode the social cues that come naturally to others.

Next step? Role-playing social scenarios. It is a safe space to practice those tricky interactions with plenty of laughs.

Role-Playing Social Scenarios

Role-playing is one of the most effective ways to help autistic teenagers improve their social interactions. It lets them practice different social situations in a safe, controlled environment, which builds comfort and familiarity—critical ingredients for real-life interactions. Through role-playing, your teen can rehearse scenarios like starting a conversation, making friends, or asking for help. The more they practice in this low-pressure setting, the more confident they will feel when faced with these real-life situations.

Choosing relevant scenarios that reflect your teen's daily life is essential. For example, you might simulate a typical day at school, where your teen engages with peers during lunch or works on a group project. Tailoring the scenarios to their needs ensures the practice feels meaningful and directly applicable to their real-world experiences. This targeted practice helps them develop the skills to navigate social settings more smoothly.

Giving constructive feedback after each role-playing session is essential. It sharpens your teen's social communication by highlighting what they did well and what needs improvement. Celebrating their achievements, like recognizing social cues or handling tough conversations, boosts their confidence and encourages positive behavior. Clear feedback highlights growth areas while affirming their strengths, keeping the process motivating rather than daunting.

Using props or scripts can make role-playing more engaging and effective. Everyday items like phones, books, or mock food can make scenarios more realistic. For instance, if you are role-playing a restaurant scene, holding a menu or a mock phone can help your teen get into the moment. Scripts provide a structure for learning how to start conversations, keep them going, and exit gracefully. These tools give your teen a clear path to follow, which can ease the anxiety that often comes with social interactions.

It is essential to create a supportive, non-judgmental environment during practice sessions. Your teen must feel free to express themselves, understanding that role-playing is for learning, not testing. When they know there is no pressure to be perfect, they will engage more and be open to trying new skills. Emphasizing progress over perfection and offering positive reinforcement helps build their self-esteem and encourages continued participation.

You can also play an essential role by modeling appropriate social behavior during the exercises. Showing how to introduce yourself, make eye contact, and listen actively gives your teen a clear example to follow. Observing these behaviors in action makes it easier for them to imitate and internalize the social skills you are teaching. Plus, it reinforces that everyone, regardless of whether they have autism, benefits from practicing social interactions.

Forming role-playing groups with peers can also be highly beneficial. Practicing with other teens creates a dynamic and diverse environment, allowing your teen to experience different types of social interactions.

Whether one-on-one conversations or group discussions, these peer-based exercises simulate real-life dynamics. Peer feedback offers valuable perspective, and hearing from others facing similar challenges can foster a sense of community and support.

Incorporating technology into role-playing offers more chances to practice. Virtual reality (VR), for example, provides immersive environments where your teen can engage with avatars in simulated social settings. For tech-savvy teens, it is an engaging and enjoyable way to practice. Virtual environments let them explore social situations independently, building skills through interactive experiences.

Your role does not end when the role-playing session is over. You can reinforce the skills your teen has learned by creating additional opportunities for practice at home. Simple activities like family game nights or casual conversations can provide excellent training for social engagement. By integrating social practice into your family's routine, the skills your teen learns during role-playing will start to feel more natural and automatic, leading to more confident interactions in the outside world.

Encouraging your teen to practice with trusted adults or siblings is another excellent way to bridge the gap between role-playing and real-world interactions. These familiar people can provide gentle guidance and support, creating a low-pressure environment where your teen feels safe to try new skills. As their confidence grows, they can expand their social interactions beyond the home.

Once your teen becomes more comfortable with role-playing, other tools, like social stories, can further enhance their understanding of social contexts. Social stories help break down social situations and offer a clear guide. Let us explore how using social stories can help strengthen your teen's social awareness even more.

Using Social Stories for Understanding Contexts

Autistic teenagers often find it difficult to understand different social contexts. Social stories can help by explaining specific social situations and showing clear examples of expected behaviors. These short narratives simplify complex interactions, making them easier to grasp. Social stories use clear language and engaging formats to explain social norms, helping your teen grasp appropriate behavior in different situations.

Creating personalized social stories is critical to keeping them relevant and engaging. Each teen has unique experiences and interests, so tailoring the stories to reflect those makes them more effective. For example, if your teen loves sports, you could create a social story around teamwork and communication on the field. This personalization helps social lessons stick because they are more relatable. The closer the stories align with your teen's daily life, the better they will internalize and apply the lessons.

After reading a social story, practicing the scenarios to strengthen the lessons is essential. Instead of simply moving on, encourage your teen to role-play the situations. This approach brings the story to life, allowing your teen to rehearse responses in a supportive environment. For instance, if the story focuses on making new friends, you can help your teen practice introducing themselves, starting conversations, and reacting to social cues. Role-playing reinforces the lessons and boosts your teen's confidence as they apply these skills in real-world interactions.

Regularly assessing the effectiveness of social stories is critical. Take time to see if they are genuinely helping your teen manage social situations more easily. Ask questions like, "Did this story make you feel more comfortable?" or "Were you able to make new friends using what we discussed?" These discussions offer helpful insights. With your teen's feedback, you can adjust the stories to keep them relevant and beneficial as they mature and their social environment shifts.

Social stories simplify complex social situations by breaking them into easy-to-follow steps. For example, a social story about attending a birthday party might guide your teen through greeting the host, joining activities, and saying goodbye. Each step includes clear dialogue and descriptions, helping your teen feel prepared and confident, which reduces anxiety and gives them a sense of control in social situations.

Personalizing social stories to reflect your teen's life makes the material more meaningful. Generic stories can feel too distant to address your teen's specific experiences. For instance, if your teen struggles with group projects at school, you could create a story focusing on teamwork and communication in a classroom setting. Using familiar names, places, and activities makes the stories more immersive and relatable, so your teen connects more deeply with the content.

Discussing and practicing social stories further strengthens the social skills your teen is learning. Reading is just the beginning; talking about the story allows your teen to ask questions and voice concerns. Practicing the scenarios afterward lets them refine their responses in a low-pressure setting. For instance, if you have read a story about handling criticism, you can practice giving feedback in different tones to prepare your teen for similar real-life situations. These rehearsals make social encounters more familiar, reducing anxiety and helping your teen respond socially appropriately.

Evaluating the effectiveness of social stories is essential for ongoing improvement. Since each teen responds differently, regular reviews and adjustments help keep the stories valid. You can observe your teen's behavior over time and track improvements in social interactions. Feedback from your teen is precious since it offers insights into how they interpret and apply the lessons. Involving your teen in this evaluation process gives them a sense of ownership over their social development.

Social stories are powerful tools that help autistic teens navigate complex social situations by breaking them down into manageable parts. They provide clarity, reduce anxiety, and build confidence. Personalizing these stories to your teen's life ensures the material stays engaging and relevant. By discussing, role-playing, and regularly evaluating these stories, you can help your teen build essential social skills.

Now that you have explored how to support your teen through social stories, let us shift focus to peer group activities. These group settings provide autistic teenagers an excellent opportunity to apply their social skills in a fun, real-world context. Here is how you can facilitate these experiences to encourage their social growth.

Facilitating Peer Group Activities

Organizing peer group activities is an effective way to help autistic teenagers develop social skills. They can connect with others and build lasting friendships by participating in structured activities. The focus should be on identifying common interests within the group to create meaningful interactions. When teens participate in activities that match their hobbies and passions, they are more likely to feel comfortable and engaged. For example, if your teen enjoys gaming, a board game night with peers who share that interest can be a perfect icebreaker. Whether it is sports, music, art, or technology, common ground creates a relaxed atmosphere, making it easier for teens to connect.

Structured activities like games, group projects, or collaborative art sessions provide a framework for social interaction. Activities with clear rules and goals reduce the anxiety some autistic teenagers might feel during free play. For instance, organizing a group project like building a model or working on a puzzle encourages teamwork and cooperation. These tasks offer natural guides for interaction, making conversations less intimidating and more focused. With a clear purpose, social exchanges feel more manageable for everyone involved.

Fostering inclusivity in peer groups is crucial. When teens feel valued, social bonds form more quickly, reducing feelings of isolation. Encouraging everyone's involvement creates a sense of belonging, regardless of social skills. Rotating roles during activities allows teens to interact with different peers and participate in all aspects of the task. This broadens their social experiences and fosters empathy within the group. Caregivers can gently remind everyone to ensure inclusion and support a welcoming environment.

Support during activities is another critical element in promoting social interaction. Support can come through verbal guidance, visual aids, or modeling behaviors. For instance, you can suggest starting or continuing a conversation during a group project. This guidance helps teens build their social skills over time. Adults can also model positive behaviors like listening attentively, taking turns, and offering feedback, which teens can observe and imitate during peer interactions.

Teaching teenagers how to resolve conflicts is also essential. Social situations often involve misunderstandings; teens must learn to handle these moments calmly. Practicing conflict resolution through role-playing can be helpful. For example, if two teens cannot agree on which game to play, you can show them how to compromise or take turns. By practicing these resolutions, teens learn how to navigate conflicts healthily, a valuable skill for maintaining friendships.

Providing feedback after activities is crucial. Discussing what went well and areas for improvement helps teens become more mindful of their social interactions. After a game night, ask questions like, "What did you enjoy most?" or "How can we make sure everyone joins in next time?" These talks promote self-awareness and reinforce positive behaviors. Feedback encourages teens to think about their actions and how they impact others.

Celebrating diversity within the group is another way to foster positive social experiences. Recognizing differences in abilities, interests, and communication styles enriches the group dynamic. For instance, a collaborative art project can showcase each teen's unique expression, reminding everyone that every contribution matters. Emphasizing diversity reduces stigma and increases acceptance, making the environment more welcoming for all participants.

Expanding structured activities outside the group can be helpful. Inclusive events like community outings or volunteer projects provide shared goals and connect autistic teens to a wider circle of peers and mentors. These experiences allow teens to practice social skills in new settings, boosting their confidence and social connections through activities like volunteering at an animal shelter or joining a neighborhood cleanup.

Technology can also support social skill development. Video modeling or visual supports can clarify group tasks, reducing uncertainty. For instance, watching a video tutorial on playing a board game can define the rules. Visual schedules and cues can also serve as helpful reminders during activities, providing structure and reducing stress.

Now that we have covered how peer group activities can promote social interaction, let us focus on another critical aspect—helping your teen develop empathy and emotional awareness. These skills can deepen their understanding of others' emotions and strengthen their social connections.

Encouraging Empathy and Emotional Awareness

Understanding and managing emotions is crucial in helping autistic teenagers develop empathy and strengthen their social relationships. When teens learn to recognize and label emotions, they build emotional intelligence. By identifying their feelings in various situations, they enhance self-awareness and find it easier to relate to others. For example, when your teen recognizes frustration during a challenging task, they start to grasp that others experience similar feelings in comparable situations. The goal is to connect their emotional experiences with those of others.

One of the most effective ways to teach empathy is by modeling it. When you respond to emotions with compassion and understanding, your teen pays attention. They see how you comfort a friend in distress or show patience when someone makes a mistake. These real-life actions have a more significant impact than just talking about empathy. By witnessing your daily practice of empathy, autistic teens begin to adopt and use those behaviors.

Perspective-taking activities are an effective way to build empathy. These exercises help your teen imagine what another person thinks or feels. You can talk about characters from books, movies, or shows and ask questions like, "What do you think made this character feel that way?" or "How would you feel in that situation?" These questions help your teen think about different perspectives and practice empathy by putting themselves in someone else's shoes, even through stories.

Nonverbal communication is essential for understanding social cues. Facial expressions, body language, and tone of voice often convey more than words. You can enhance your teen's social awareness by teaching them to identify these signals. Make it engaging by people-watching at a park or mall and discussing their body language. Playing charades, where your teen acts out emotions silently, also helps them notice nonverbal signals. These activities make learning fun while highlighting the value of understanding unspoken communication.

Structured role-playing is another effective strategy for autistic teens to practice social skills. In a controlled environment, they can act out different social scenarios without the pressure of real-world consequences. You can make these role-playing sessions more engaging by using props or simple scripts. Props provide visual context, helping your teen better understand the situation. At the same time, scripts allow them to rehearse how they would respond in various scenarios. This practice builds their confidence and social competence, helping them feel more prepared for future interactions.

Creating a safe and supportive home environment is critical to teaching emotional awareness and empathy. Establish clear household rules affirming emotions, such as "It is okay to feel anything." This helps your teen express themselves without fear of being judged. You can also build family routines prioritizing emotional honesty, like regular check-ins where everyone shares their feelings. Posting a feelings chart in a visible spot constantly reminds everyone to recognize and respect each other's emotions.

Community service is another effective way to foster empathy. Volunteering as a family introduces your teen to new environments and shifts their focus to helping others. It provides practical opportunities to understand various perspectives. After volunteering, have family discussions about what everyone learned and how it felt to offer support. This reflection strengthens empathy and deepens family bonds as you contribute to the community.

As a parent or caregiver, you have countless opportunities to be an empathetic role model—whether at home, school, or community. Each time you demonstrate empathy, you are showing your teen how to apply it in their own life. Reinforce empathetic behaviors with praise and encouragement whenever your teen shows consideration for others. This positive reinforcement boosts their confidence and helps solidify these behaviors over time.

Discussing current events is another valuable tool for teaching empathy. Whether it is local news or global stories, these discussions allow your teen to explore beyond their immediate experiences and think about how others might feel in different situations. When you talk about these events, focus on the feelings of those involved. This makes the issues more relatable and helps your teen connect emotionally to what is happening in the world around them.

Remember, developing empathy is a process that takes time. Your teen is constantly growing, and their capacity for empathy will expand with practice and guidance. Every interaction offers a teachable moment, so staying patient and attentive to these opportunities is critical. By embracing these practices, you equip your teen with the emotional intelligence they need to build meaningful relationships and confidently navigate social interactions.

Key Takeaways

- Your autistic teen can learn and improve social skills through role-playing and practice.

- Role-playing offers autistic teens a secure space to practice social interactions.

- A supportive, judgment-free environment encourages full participation in social practice.

- Modeling appropriate social behavior gives teens a clear example to follow.

- Social stories teach teens how to navigate complex social situations by breaking them down into more straightforward, manageable steps.

- Peer group activities with shared interests create opportunities for meaningful social interaction.

- Conflict resolution and feedback after activities help teens improve social awareness.

- Teaching nonverbal communication is vital for interpreting social cues.

- Volunteering and community service help teens focus on others' needs and build empathy.

- Discussing current events can expand teens' emotional awareness and connection to others.

As you guide your teen through social growth, you also consider their educational journey. Supporting their learning and finding the right resources can feel overwhelming, but you are not alone. In the next chapter, we will look at how to support their academic needs, helping them succeed in school and life.

Chapter 4:

Educational Pathways and Support

You have spent hours researching educational options for your autistic teen, trying to crack the code of which path fits best. Public school? Private school? Homeschooling? You have considered them all, even had dreams of your teen opening the first school for "just-right" education. But let us be honest—it is a journey full of trial and error, often involving last-minute emails to teachers and an unhealthy amount of coffee. You are not alone, though. With the proper support, these pathways can lead to success.

Now, speaking of support, let us talk about Individualized Education Plans—your secret weapon for navigating school with more confidence.

Individualized Education Plans

Individualized Education Programs (IEPs) are essential for creating tailored educational experiences for autistic teenagers. These legally binding documents outline specific academic goals and services to ensure each student gets the support needed to succeed academically and socially. Schools are held accountable for providing services like specialized instruction, assistive technology, or curriculum modifications outlined in the IEP.

As a parent, your role in IEP meetings is essential. Your deep understanding of your child is crucial in an effective educational plan. Sharing your perspective ensures your teen's goals are practical and attainable. For example, suggest strategies that work well at home and adapt them for school. You can also advocate for accommodations like extended time on tests or quiet spaces for sensory breaks—details that school staff might overlook.

Regular review meetings keep the IEP up-to-date with your teen's progress. These meetings allow the IEP team to assess your child's growth and adjust goals accordingly. For example, if your teen masters a math concept beforehand, the goals can shift to more challenging material. On the other hand, if social skills remain a challenge, the IEP can be updated to provide more targeted support, such as a peer buddy system or additional social skills training. Autism Behavior Services, Inc. (2023) highlights how this flexibility ensures the IEP evolves with your child's needs.

Disagreements between parents and schools about IEP content or implementation are not unusual, but mediation can help resolve conflicts. Mediation provides a neutral environment where both parties can openly discuss their concerns and find a compromise. For example, suppose you believe your teen is not getting enough speech therapy. In that case, a mediator can facilitate a conversation to adjust the services without escalating to a formal complaint. According to the U.S. Department of Education, mediation is available under the Individuals with Disabilities Education Act (IDEA). It helps avoid the stress of due process hearings (*Mediation*, 2017).

The IEP is a legal safeguard to ensure your teenager receives the necessary accommodations and modifications under IDEA. Schools must provide tailored services, such as noise-canceling headphones for sensory sensitivities or breaks for sensory overload. Documenting these supports in the IEP holds the school accountable for delivering a free and appropriate public education.

The IEP team reviews the plan at least once a year to ensure it stays aligned with your teen's needs. The team celebrates and sets new goals if your teen shows significant progress, such as improved social communication skills. Suppose your teen does not meet the milestones. In that case, the team discusses new strategies, like role-playing activities or adding speech therapy sessions. This annual review keeps the IEP relevant and effective.

Mediation is critical in maintaining a positive relationship between parents and schools. When disagreements arise, it offers a way to communicate and find solutions openly. For example, suppose you feel the school is not implementing the IEP correctly. In that case, a mediator can help you and the school collaborate to address the issue. Mediation resolves conflicts at the moment and strengthens trust for future interactions.

IEPs offer a structured approach to tracking educational progress. Goals are crafted based on assessments and input from teachers, therapists, and parents, ensuring they are measurable and attainable. For example, suppose your teen is working on self-regulation. In that case, the IEP might set goals for the student to practice breathing exercises when feeling overwhelmed. These clear objectives allow everyone to track progress and adjust the plan.

As a parent, you play a critical role in the IEP process. Your unique perspective on your teen's strengths and challenges helps ensure the educational plan is genuinely individualized. For example, suppose visual schedules work well at home. In that case, you can suggest incorporating them into the school day to provide consistency. Your advocacy helps ensure the plan supports your teen's academic and social growth.

The IEP review process is dynamic, allowing the team to adjust goals or services quickly if your teen is not progressing as expected. Regular reviews help ensure the IEP remains focused on your child's success and evolves as they grow.

Now that you understand the IEP process, let us look at the next critical phase: transition planning. As your autistic teenager approaches adulthood, this part of the IEP becomes crucial in helping them prepare for life after high school, whether aiming for college, vocational training, or independent living.

Transition Planning in Schools

Transition planning is essential for preparing autistic teenagers for adulthood, mapping out their future paths to help them succeed. Starting as early as age 14—or even earlier, depending on the Individualized Education Program (IEP) team's recommendations—aligns with educational guidelines and gives your teen time to build crucial skills.

Transition planning requires focusing on education, employment, and independent living skills. It is a holistic approach that ensures your teen's growth in all areas, making them more independent. Educational goals should not only focus on academics and life skills like managing money, time, and social situations. Goals could include exploring career options, understanding workplace dynamics, and learning job-specific skills. Independent living skills range from cooking and cleaning to managing healthcare and transportation.

Teachers and counselors are crucial here, introducing your teen to vocational training programs and job resources tailored to their strengths. For example, if your teen is tech-savvy, a counselor might suggest a technology-focused vocational course or help them find an internship. Your teen gains practical skills and hands-on learning through these experiences.

Family involvement is equally important. Your insights into your teen's strengths, challenges, and preferences help create a more tailored plan. As a parent, you can set realistic goals, celebrate progress, and offer encouragement during tough times. Research highlights that teenagers with strong family support are likelier to reach their education and employment goals (Day, 2010). Family involvement fosters a sense of shared responsibility and unity, which reassures your teen as they navigate the complexities of adulthood.

Starting transition planning around age 16 gives your teen ample time to explore various options, adjust their goals, and develop essential skills (Lee, n.d.). This approach eases the pressure of transitioning into adulthood. Early planning also provides time to tackle challenges and ensure they receive support.

An effective transition plan sets measurable goals and incorporates periodic check-ins to track improvement. Setting specific objectives, such as submitting job applications or developing life skills, gives your teen a clear path forward. Consistent assessments show where additional support might be necessary. For example, if time management proves difficult, you can adjust the plan to include more resources. Goal-setting and progress tracking significantly improve the chances of successful transitions into adulthood for autistic teens.

Teachers, counselors, and families collaborate to achieve the same goals. They hold regular meetings to provide feedback and make necessary changes to the plan. Teachers and counselors bring professional expertise while you provide personal insights, making the plan more effective.

Vocational training and job resources are essential in preparing your teen for adulthood. Programs in various fields, from trades to the arts, offer practical experience. In contrast, resources like internships and mentorship programs expose them to the working world. Research shows that students with disabilities who participate in vocational education have better employment outcomes than those who do not (Harvey, 2001).

Independent living skills, like budgeting, cooking, and self-care, are equally important. These can be taught in school or through after-school programs. Teaching your teen self-advocacy—how to make decisions and stand up for their rights—helps them take control as they move into adulthood.

A transition plan must be flexible for success. As your teen's strengths and interests change, adjust the plan accordingly. Periodically reviewing it ensures it stays relevant and matches their evolving goals.

With transition planning, your teen gets the foundation they need for adulthood. Another crucial part of the solution is implementing specialized learning programs. These programs take a personalized approach to education, addressing the unique academic, social, and emotional needs of autistic teenagers to support their growth further.

Specialized Learning Programs

Specialized learning programs tailored for autistic teenagers are critical in supporting their unique needs, helping them grow in key areas vital for their personal development and independence. These programs provide targeted support, nurturing growth in social skills, life skills, and job readiness. With individualized approaches, they meet teens where they are, empowering them to succeed in school and beyond.

Types of Specialized Programs

Several specialized learning programs focus on different aspects of a teen's growth. For instance, social skills training programs focus on teaching teens how to interact with others effectively. This is important for making friends, succeeding in school, and navigating workplace environments. These programs often incorporate role-playing, group activities, and direct instruction, helping teens practice social cues, body language, and responses in various social settings. Research shows that social skills training significantly improves peer relationships and reduces feelings of isolation in autistic teenagers, a key outcome for their long-term emotional well-being (Hotton & Coles, 2016).

Life skills classes equip autistic teenagers with the tools they need for independent living. These classes teach various skills, from basic tasks like cooking and cleaning to more advanced ones like managing finances, solving problems, and making decisions. Learning these skills boosts teens' confidence and self-sufficiency and smooths the transition to adulthood. Life skills training promotes independence and lowers stress for teens and their caregivers.

Vocational programs aim to prepare teens for the workforce, focusing on job-specific skills, interview techniques, and workplace etiquette. Autistic teens can participate in internships or job shadowing to gain practical experience. These experiences help them learn workplace expectations and provide a sense of purpose and achievement. According to Autism Speaks, about 42% of young adults with autism remain unemployed, highlighting the importance of vocational programs that give teens a better shot at finding meaningful employment (*Autism in the Workforce*, 2021).

Benefits of Specialized Learning

Specialized programs often emphasize personalized learning, which tailors education to each teen's needs. This ensures the lessons are appropriately challenging, helping teens progress without becoming frustrated or bored. Personalization considers the unique strengths and challenges of each autistic teenager. For example, while one teen might excel with visual aids, another might learn better through auditory instructions. Personalized learning approaches increase engagement and help teens reach their full potential as they feel more in control of their learning experience.

Additionally, these programs create a structured and predictable environment, which is essential for many autistic teens who may struggle with anxiety or a fear of change. The consistency provided by specialized programs can significantly reduce stress, allowing teens to focus on learning and development. Teachers and instructors in these programs are often specifically trained to understand the needs of autistic teenagers, allowing them to provide the proper support at the right time. For example, some instructors may use visual schedules or sensory breaks to accommodate a teen's sensory needs, making the learning process smoother.

Finding the Right Program

When selecting a specialized learning program for your teen, it is essential to consider their strengths, interests, and challenges. You will want to assess which areas require the most support and what type of environment will help them thrive. Visiting potential programs and talking to instructors can give you valuable insights. Involving your teen in decision-making is equally important, as their comfort with the program can significantly impact its effectiveness. For instance, if your teen feels excited or at ease with a particular program, they are more likely to engage and benefit from it.

Another crucial factor is the program's flexibility. Autistic teens do not follow a one-size-fits-all approach to learning, so the program should offer customization based on ongoing assessments. Flexible programs that adjust to a teen's evolving needs tend to have better long-term outcomes in both academic and personal growth.

Measuring Success

Tracking progress in any specialized program is essential. You and the instructors should work together to set clear, achievable goals for your teen from the beginning. Regularly conducting formal and informal assessments will demonstrate whether you are meeting those goals and identify areas that need adjustments. For example, if a teaching method is not practical, you can adjust it based on your teen's feedback and progress reports. Open communication between parents, instructors, and your teen ensures the learning environment stays supportive and responsive to their needs.

Success is not only about academic achievement. For many autistic teens, progress in social interactions, independence, and self-confidence holds just as much value. Seeing your teen improve communication skills, connect more with peers, or take on new responsibilities at home shows growth. Recognizing even small achievements can lift your teen's self-esteem and help them feel proud.

Understanding the variety of specialized learning programs available for your autistic teen is just the first step. Next, we will examine these programs' strategies for fostering your teen's growth. These strategies can significantly impact your teen's progress and overall experience, helping you make more informed decisions about which program might best fit.

Collaboration With Educators and Support Staff

Building strong relationships with educators and support staff is critical to creating effective educational pathways for autistic teenagers. The foundations of these relationships are clear communication, collaboration, understanding of the resources available, and specialized training for educators. Teens benefit from a more supportive and individualized learning environment when everyone works together.

First and foremost, open and regular communication between parents, educators, and support staff is vital. When communication stays consistent, it fosters trust and ensures that everyone is committed to the teen's success. This can take the form of regular check-ins, emails, or even casual conversations to keep everyone updated on the teen's progress, challenges, and achievements. For example, a simple email chain can be an easy way to ensure everyone is on the same page, addressing concerns as they arise. Studies show that school-family solid partnerships can improve student outcomes, especially for those with special needs (Smith et al., 2020). Consistent communication helps align approaches across home and school environments, making identifying potential issues easier and adjusting strategies as needed.

Team meetings are another critical aspect of maintaining communication. These meetings offer a structured space to discuss challenges and brainstorm solutions. They foster collaborative problem-solving by bringing teachers, aides, therapists, and parents together. Each team member provides their perspective on how to support the autistic teenager best, resulting in a more comprehensive and effective plan. For instance, a team meeting might help educators and parents identify new strategies or accommodations if a teenager struggles with a specific part of their curriculum. This could involve incorporating tools like visual schedules or offering alternative assignments that cater to the teen's strengths. Collaborative planning significantly enhances student engagement and progress in school. Regular monthly or quarterly meetings ensure that all parties are aligned and the teen's needs are at the forefront of decision-making.

In addition to communication and collaboration, understanding the school's available resources is essential. Schools often offer services such as counseling, special education programs, and extracurricular activities tailored to students with autism. Parents and teachers must stay knowledgeable about these opportunities to champion proper use. For example, sensory rooms can provide autistic teenagers with a safe space to decompress when overwhelmed, helping them refocus on their learning. Knowing about these resources allows parents to push for accommodations that make the learning environment more suitable. If your teen struggles with sensory overload, requesting access to these accommodations can significantly enhance their experience at school.

You should work with the school to adjust the classroom environment or request extra support during exams. For example, some autistic teens benefit from extended time or a quieter space during tests. Understanding your child's rights and the school's available resources enables you to make sure they receive the support they need. Working with the IEP team also helps ensure the educational plan addresses the teen's needs.

Specialized training for educators is another pillar in building a solid support system. Teachers who complete autism-specific training can more effectively tailor their instruction to meet the needs of students with autism. Training programs cover behavioral interventions, personalized teaching methods, and ways to foster an inclusive classroom environment. For example, a teacher who has completed this training might use more visual aids or establish a consistent daily schedule, which can benefit autistic teenagers. This ensures that your teen learns in surroundings that comprehend and cater to their conditions.

For instance, imagine you regularly communicate with your teen's teachers through weekly updates. During a quarterly team meeting, you mention that your teen struggles with group work. The teachers might suggest using a sensory room to help your teen decompress before group activities. Meanwhile, the school's occupational therapist at the meeting might recommend incorporating short sensory breaks throughout the day to help regulate the teen's emotions. This collaborative approach addresses the issue and provides a personalized solution that benefits your teen.

Key Takeaways

- Individualized Education Programs (IEPs) offer personalized educational plans for autistic teens, ensuring they obtain the required help.

- Parents play a crucial role in shaping and advocating for their teen's IEP goals, ensuring they are realistic and achievable.

- Transition planning, which starts at age 14, prepares autistic teens for adulthood by focusing on education, employment, and independent living skills.

- Vocational programs and job resources are vital in helping autistic teens gain hands-on work experience and improve employment outcomes.

- Specialized learning programs offer targeted support in social skills, life skills, and job readiness, tailored to meet teens' unique needs.

- Personalized learning in specialized programs increases engagement and reduces frustration, helping teens reach their full potential.

- Collaboration between parents, educators, and support staff ensures a consistent approach. It creates a supportive learning environment for autistic teens.

Now that you have clearly understood specialized learning programs and their impact, it is time to focus on the next crucial step: preparing your teen for the workforce. Employment readiness and career planning are vital in helping them build skills and confidence for a fulfilling future.

Chapter 5:

Employment Readiness and Career Planning

Imagine this: Your autistic teen is getting ready for their first part-time job interview. They have practiced their handshake, nailed their introduction, and even got the outfit right—only to realize that, midway through the interview, they start talking about their love for space, even though the job is at a local café. You chuckle because it is so "them." But the important thing? They showed up, ready to take that first step toward employment. Career planning is rarely straightforward, but it is always a learning process.

Now that they are dipping their toes into employment readiness, let us talk about identifying strengths and interests—because that is where real growth begins.

Identifying Strengths and Interests

Helping your autistic teen recognize their strengths and interests is a critical step in career planning. When they clearly understand their unique skills and passions, they are better equipped to start a fulfilling career that aligns with their abilities and interests.

Assessing Strengths: Using Tools and Observations

Start by assessing your teen's strengths through both formal assessments and everyday observations. Several tools can help with this, such as interest inventories, aptitude tests, and personality tests. For example, the 16Personalities test can offer insights into your teen's natural tendencies and potential career paths.

Observing your teen in various situations can provide valuable insights. Notice when they seem most excited or absorbed in an activity. These moments can disclose valuable insights about their interests and strengths. This process helps create a more straightforward path for them—whether it is a love for animals that could lead to a career in veterinary science or an affinity for technology that might point to programming or engineering.

Encouraging your teen to be self-aware is equally essential. When they recognize their skills and what they enjoy, they gain confidence. That confidence becomes crucial in helping them realize how their strengths can apply to a career. Celebrate their achievements, no matter how small, and help them recognize how these wins contribute to their future skill development.

Exploring Occupations With the Right Tools

Once you have a good sense of your teen's strengths and interests, it is time to explore potential career options. Fortunately, many tools are available to assist with this. Websites like CareerOneStop and U.S. Department of Labor resources have many career exploration features. These platforms let teens search for jobs, learn about their needed skills, and understand salary expectations.

Interactive experiences like job shadowing, volunteering, or even online career simulations can also be a great way to explore different fields. These real-world experiences give your teen a clearer idea of what specific jobs involve without the pressure of commitment. For example, they can see if working with animals, coding software, or managing a small project feels right for them.

You must ensure the career exploration process stays engaging and tailored to your teen's needs. Combining online tools with real-life experiences can help your teen feel empowered rather than overwhelmed.

Creating a Profile to Highlight Skills and Interests

Once you have helped your teen identify their strengths and interests, it is time to help them create a profile that showcases these abilities. This profile will be beneficial when applying for jobs or internships. It should highlight their skills, educational background, hobbies, and any work or volunteer experience they have gained.

Encouraging your teen to build a resume and even an online portfolio can be helpful at this stage. They can include examples of projects, artwork, coding samples, or other work they have done. Platforms like LinkedIn are excellent for creating a professional presence and networking with potential employers.

This profile does not just serve as a tool for job searches. It also builds your teen's confidence by affirming their abilities. Plus, it provides a clear, organized way to present their talents and experiences to future employers. Working together will ensure their profile feels authentic and highlights their unique qualities.

Setting Goals Based on Interests

Once your teen has a better idea of their strengths and interests, it is time to help them set goals. These objectives provide guidance and encouragement, helping them stay focused on their chosen career path.

Start with small, manageable goals. Maybe they will complete a course, volunteer, or attend a workshop in a field they are interested in. Short-term goals act as steps that lead to larger career aspirations. Regularly reviewing and adjusting these goals can also help as your teen gains new experiences and their interests evolve.

It is important to remind your teen that career paths are rarely straightforward. Changes in goals are natural, and it is part of their growth process. Sharing examples of successful people with diverse career journeys can help ease the pressure of choosing the "perfect" path immediately. Encourage them to stay open to new opportunities as they develop.

Practical Advice for Parents

To support your teen through this process, remember to:

- **Be supportive, not pushy:** Encourage your teen's exploration without dictating their choices. Keep the conversation open about their dreams and aspirations.

- **Expose them to diverse activities:** Get your teen involved in extracurriculars like sports, clubs, or community service to help them discover new talents.

- **Lead by example:** Show them that pursuing passions is possible. If you enjoy your work or hobbies, they will see that it is attainable for them, too.

- **Use available resources:** Utilize school counselors, career centers, and online tools to guide your teen with professional advice.

Now that your teen understands their strengths and interests better, the next step is to help them navigate job coaching and mentorship. These can provide invaluable support as they continue their career journey.

Job Coaching and Mentorship

Job coaching and mentorship play a crucial role in helping autistic teens get ready for the workforce. These resources provide essential guidance and encouragement, assisting teens to build the skills necessary to handle adult work environments. Job coaches specializing in supporting individuals with disabilities, including autism, help teens develop the workplace skills essential for success. They guide teens through job tasks, teaching them to adjust to various work settings and meet job expectations. Coaches help teens strengthen critical soft skills, such as problem-solving, teamwork, and communication, which are vital for success in any workplace. By tailoring their approach, job coaches address each teen's unique strengths, interests, and needs. This personalized support boosts teens' confidence and competence in managing job responsibilities.

Mentorship is another powerful tool for autistic teens as they prepare for employment. Families are encouraged to seek mentors who can provide insights into specific industries and help teens build their professional networks. Mentors can draw from their experiences, provide career guidance, and help teens explore various career paths. The Office of Disability and Employment Policy highlights that career-focused mentors are critical in helping young people understand the world of work, offering practical advice, and even serving as references. This guidance allows teens to envision their future careers and learn the steps necessary to achieve their goals.

Training teens in essential skills is one of the most critical steps in preparing them for the workforce. This training should go beyond job-specific tasks to include crucial life skills, such as responsibility, communication, and professionalism. Teaching responsibility involves showing teens how to manage their time, prioritize tasks, and meet deadlines, which are vital in any job. Training in interpersonal skills is just as essential as it teaches teens how to communicate clearly, listen attentively, and work well with colleagues. Professionalism includes understanding workplace etiquette, dressing correctly, and keeping a positive attitude.

The Office of Disability and Employment Policy developed programs like "Skills to Pay the Bills: Mastering Soft Skills for Workplace Success," which provide valuable resources for teens to build these essential skills. These programs help teens develop the practical skills needed for employment success, setting them up for smoother transitions into the workforce.

Advocacy is another essential skill for autistic teens to develop. Knowing how to advocate for themselves in the workplace—whether requesting accommodations or expressing their needs—helps them succeed professionally. Mentors can be invaluable in teaching teens how to communicate their needs confidently and advocate for the support they require. When teens assert themselves and understand their rights, they handle workplace challenges more confidently and independently.

The benefits of job coaching and mentorship go far beyond acquiring skills. These supports help teens build self-esteem and resilience, which are critical for long-term success in any career. Structured programs provide opportunities for teens to practice their skills in real-world environments, with guidance from professionals and peers. Studies have shown that teens participating in such programs report improved job skills, communication, and employment readiness (*Benefits of Mentoring*, n.d.).

Families have an essential part in supporting this journey. Encouraging teens to participate in skill-building programs, seeking out mentors, and reinforcing the importance of soft skills at home can amplify the impact of formal training. Open communication between families, job coaches, and mentors creates a robust support system that helps address each teen's unique needs, ensuring they are well-prepared for employment.

Now that we have explored the value of job coaching and mentorship, let us focus on the next crucial step: gaining work experience. Work opportunities reinforce these skills and give teens a sense of independence and accomplishment.

Work Experience Opportunities

In today's fast-paced job market, getting practical work experience early on is critical to helping teens prepare for their future careers. Teens gain valuable hands-on experience through internships and volunteer opportunities, which help them build resumes and develop essential skills. These experiences allow teenagers to create a solid work ethic, practice time management, and remember to collaborate in a real-world environment.

High school internships, or those taken after graduation, offer learning opportunities beyond the classroom. Many companies offer internship programs for teens and young adults, allowing them to explore different careers. For example, the National Park Service provides paid internships where teens gain hands-on experience in conservation and environmental education. These internships help teens learn about workplace dynamics, explore various career options, and start building professional connections that can benefit their future.

Volunteer roles are another great way to prepare teens for the workforce. Volunteering helps develop life skills like responsibility, communication, and empathy. Teens can gain valuable work experience while making meaningful contributions to their communities. For example, teens who volunteer at local shelters, community centers, or non-profits gain skills that make them more appealing to future employers.

Job shadowing is another excellent way for teens to explore career options. Spending a day observing a professional allows them to see firsthand what different jobs entail. Teens can ask questions and understand whether the role matches their strengths and interests. This type of experience benefits teens who are not sure which career path to pursue, as it provides a clearer picture of what specific jobs involve without requiring a long-term commitment.

Teens with unique skills or interests may find entrepreneurship an exciting option. Starting a small business or freelance venture allows teens to hone essential entrepreneurial skills like problem-solving, creativity, and financial management. Whether selling handmade products, tutoring services, or launching an online store, entrepreneurship teaches independence and fosters innovation. Access to online platforms and resources gives teens more opportunities to start businesses and gain experience.

Programs specifically designed to provide valuable work experience to autistic teens are also available. Programs like Arc Broward's School of

Hire Education focus on career education and community-based learning for students with developmental disabilities. These programs equip teens with the skills necessary for independent living and future employment. Additionally, Youth Links provides experiential learning and skill-building opportunities that prepare teens for post-secondary education and the workforce.

One practical tool parents can create with their teens is a strengths-based profile. This profile showcases your teen's skills, interests, and achievements, making it useful when they apply for jobs. Including real examples of their strengths can show potential employers how capable and talented your teen is, helping them stand out in the application process.

For teens interested in public service and conservation, programs like the Youth Conservation Corps offer summer jobs focused on environmental education and conservation projects. These programs allow teens to work on noteworthy tasks and earn compensation. These ventures strengthen their resumes and help them develop a sense of responsibility for preserving natural and cultural heritage.

Federal internship programs like the Pathways Program are also great options for teens exploring government careers. These internships offer paid positions and provide experience in a variety of fields. Completing these programs can help teens land permanent federal jobs, giving them a head start in their careers.

Encouraging teens to explore different types of work experiences is essential for helping them discover their passions and develop the skills they need for success. As a parent or caregiver, supporting your teen in finding internships, volunteer roles, job shadowing opportunities, or even starting their own business is a great way to help them prepare for the future. Specialized programs designed for autistic teens can provide additional support, ensuring they are ready to enter the workforce with confidence and independence.

Now that your teen is exploring different work experiences, the next step is preparing them for interviews and understanding workplace accommodations. Let us dive into what you can do to help your teen feel confident and supported as they navigate the job application process.

Interview Preparation and Workplace Accommodations

Preparing autistic teens for the workforce involves several key steps. Job interview readiness and understanding workplace accommodations are among the most crucial. You can take practical steps to help your teen gain confidence and understand their rights, ensuring a smoother transition into employment.

One effective strategy is role-playing interview scenarios. This approach lets your teen practice answering common interview questions in a low-pressure environment. You can play the role of the interviewer, asking typical questions like, "Tell me about yourself" or "Why do you want this job?" This practice will help your teen develop thoughtful responses. Reviewing mock interviews, especially if you record them, can give you insight into areas needing improvement. Encourage your teen to hold eye contact, listen attentively, and display confident body language. These simple yet impactful adjustments help them feel more at ease and strengthen their communication skills.

Another crucial part of preparation is teaching your teen the importance of professional appearance. First impressions are vital, especially in a job interview. You can help your teen choose suitable attire, explaining that dressing neatly reflects professionalism and seriousness about the job. Even small advice, like wearing clean clothes, practicing good hygiene, and picking appropriate shoes, can significantly influence their perception. You can also explain the idea of dressing "one step above" the expected dress code to show enthusiasm and respect for the opportunity.

A vital part of this process is ensuring your teen understands their rights under the Americans with Disabilities Act (ADA). The ADA guarantees that individuals with disabilities, including autistic teenagers, have the right to request reasonable accommodations in the workplace. Make sure your teen knows they have the right to request accommodations that will help them perform their job more effectively. These accommodations could include a modified work schedule, assistive technology, or a quiet workspace to help manage sensory sensitivities. However, it is crucial to emphasize that disclosing a disability is a personal decision, and your teen should feel comfortable with the process if they believe it will support their success at work.

You can guide your teen through disclosure as a parent or caregiver. They must know employers cannot ask about disabilities before extending a job offer. You can reassure your teen that the ADA protects them and help them decide when and how to disclose their autism, if at all. When they learn about these rights, they gain the confidence to handle challenges and speak up for their needs.

In terms of support, many organizations offer resources to help with interview preparation and understanding workplace accommodations. The Job Accommodation Network (JAN) offers free, confidential guidance on accommodations and the ADA. This can be a great resource if your teen needs specific accommodations or advice navigating the disclosure process. The Equal Employment Opportunity Commission (EEOC) enforces ADA protections and provides educational materials on disability prejudice. You can also connect with the ADA National Network, which provides information and training on disability rights and accommodations through its regional centers. These resources offer valuable support for you and your teen as they prepare to enter the workforce.

Goal-setting can also motivate your teen as they work toward interview readiness and job opportunities. Encourage them to set short-term goals, such as participating in mock interviews, and long-term goals, like securing a part-time job. Breaking these larger goals into smaller, manageable steps helps make the process feel more achievable. For instance, if your teen is interested in customer service, they can start by researching job openings, then work on crafting a resume, practicing interview skills, and eventually applying. Each step builds toward their goal, and celebrating small victories helps maintain their motivation.

Finally, encouraging self-advocacy is crucial. Encourage your teen to practice asking for accommodations, like flexible work hours or noise-canceling headphones, to help manage sensory sensitivities. Role-playing these scenarios can boost their confidence when communicating their needs in real work situations. By teaching your teens how to advocate for themselves respectfully and assertively, you are setting them up to thrive in the workplace.

Key Takeaways

- Help autistic teens recognize their strengths and interests to guide career planning.

- Use assessments and observations to identify their natural skills and passions.

- Encourage self-awareness and celebrate small achievements to build confidence.

- Develop a resume or profile emphasizing your teen's strengths to showcase their skills and experiences.

- Set realistic goals aligning with their interests and adjust them as they gain more experience.

- Support job exploration through internships, volunteering, and entrepreneurship.

- Job coaching and mentorship can help develop workplace skills and confidence.

- Prepare for interviews through role-playing, focusing on communication and appearance.

- Educate teens on their workplace rights and accommodations under the ADA.

- Encourage self-advocacy in requesting accommodations and understanding workplace needs.

- Use available resources like the Job Accommodation Network for guidance and support.

As your teen starts navigating the working world, keeping them healthy and balanced becomes even more critical. Managing stress, staying active, and practicing self-care can significantly affect their well-being. Let us talk about how you can support their health management and self-care.

Chapter 6:

Health Management and Self-Care

You observe your teen stack all their vitamins next to their water bottle as if it is a puzzle they are determined to solve. "Mom, do these even work?" they ask, eyebrows raised. You chuckle, thinking about how often you have asked yourself the same thing. "Well, they cannot hurt," you say, reminding them how important balance is. Between sensory overload and the roller coaster of emotions, health management and self-care are not just buzzwords; they are lifelines. You are learning that one-size-fits-all wellness plans do not apply here.

Speaking of lifelines, keeping up with routine medical care can make a huge difference in your teen's overall well-being.

Routine Medical Care and Checkups

Regular medical checkups play a vital role in ensuring your autistic teen stays healthy, especially as they transition into adulthood. These visits are not just routine—they help track developmental progress, manage ongoing health concerns, and offer early intervention when needed.

One significant benefit of these checkups is monitoring your teen's growth and development. During annual exams, doctors check important metrics like height, weight, and body mass index (BMI), which can reveal potential health concerns. Addressing issues early allows for timely interventions. For example, if a doctor detects a nutritional deficiency, they can recommend dietary adjustments that support better development.

A crucial aspect of health management for autistic teens is establishing a "medical home." This goes beyond having a regular doctor. It involves creating a coordinated care plan covering all health-related needs, ensuring that care is more comprehensive and easier to navigate. This continuity makes it easier to communicate with specialists and ensures that care is more comprehensive. A dedicated healthcare provider who knows your teen's history can offer personalized care, providing immediate support and proactive health planning for the future.

Health screenings and vaccinations are other essential components of these appointments. Screenings like blood pressure and cholesterol tests help identify early risk factors for chronic conditions such as heart disease or diabetes. Vaccinations keep your teen protected from diseases, which is especially important for autistic individuals who may have more vulnerable immune systems. Staying up-to-date on immunizations also helps prevent outbreaks, benefiting your teen and the broader community.

Medical appointments can often feel overwhelming for autistic teens, but using visual aids and schedules can ease their anxiety. Tools like illustrated guides or videos that explain what to expect during checkups, a visual schedule that outlines each step of the visit, and social stories depicting positive experiences at the doctor's office can all make the process less intimidating and more manageable for your teen.

Regular checkups have several benefits, including the relief and reassurance that comes with early diagnosis of potential health issues. Healthcare providers review your teen's medical history during these exams and perform a thorough physical assessment. By identifying concerns early, you can help prevent complications. For instance, if doctors catch scoliosis or vision problems early, they can provide the necessary treatment for your teen, ultimately improving their quality of life.

Establishing a medical home also helps foster a trusting relationship with a healthcare provider who understands your teen's needs. This personalized approach allows the provider to develop care plans tailored to your teen's specific challenges, and they can act as a central coordinator for any specialists involved in your teen's care. Having a single point of contact for all medical concerns makes navigating the healthcare system easier, reducing stress for you as a caregiver.

Vaccinations and screenings are preventive and vital in supporting your teen's long-term health and development. Routine screenings help doctors catch risk factors early, allowing for timely interventions to prevent chronic conditions later on. Following recommended vaccination schedules protects your teen from preventable diseases, keeping them healthier overall. By scheduling these checkups, you actively safeguard their well-being.

If your teen feels anxious about medical visits, implementing visual aids and schedules can significantly reduce their discomfort. These tools help your teen understand the appointment steps and reduce fear by showing them what to expect. Using social stories to depict positive doctor visits helps normalize the experience and makes it less intimidating. With a clear schedule that outlines each phase of the visit, you can provide structure, giving your teen a sense of control and making the process much more manageable.

As you continue to focus on your teen's physical health, do not forget that mental health is just as important. Finding the right resources can help you support your teen's emotional well-being, offering the guidance and tools they need to thrive.

Mental Health Resources

Recognizing mental health issues in autistic teenagers is essential for early intervention and ongoing support. As a parent or caregiver, you can observe your teen's behavior and spot anything unusual. Autistic teens may find it harder to express their emotions verbally, so mental health struggles often appear through subtle changes. You might notice increased irritability, withdrawal from favorite activities, or sleep and eating patterns shifts. Perceptiveness to sensory intakes, like noise or glow, often indicates your teen is anxious or stressed. By staying alert to these changes, you can address issues before they become overwhelming, empowering you to support your teen's emotional well-being.

Open and consistent communication with your teen is vital in identifying potential concerns. Even if your teen is not directly discussing how they feel, your support can encourage them to express emotions in other ways. Observing behavior over time helps you differentiate between normal mood swings and something that requires more attention. Learning about signs of anxiety and depression enables you to catch early warning signs and know when it is time to seek help.

Connecting with mental health professionals is the next step if you notice concerning signs. It is essential to find a therapist experienced with autistic teens, as they will understand your teen's unique challenges and can tailor techniques accordingly. Start by consulting your pediatrician for recommendations or researching specialists. When you encounter a possible therapist, ask about their treatment technique, background with autism, and how they adjust therapies to fit individual needs. Establishing a solid relationship with the therapist and maintaining regular appointments ensures consistent support, with flexible treatment plans as your teen's needs evolve.

Cognitive behavioral therapy (CBT) helps individuals change harmful thinking patterns and behaviors. It is proven effective for teens dealing with anxiety and depression. For those who struggle socially, social skills training can provide valuable tools for improving interactions and reducing isolation. Discussing these options with your teen's therapist helps you tailor a treatment plan to their needs and strengths.

Community resources, alongside therapy, significantly contribute to supporting mental health. Many local organizations provide counseling, recreational activities, and support groups for autistic teens and their families. These gatherings provide an area where parents can communicate guidance, offer encouragement, and discover emotional support for their teenagers. National institutions, such as the National Alliance on Mental Illness (NAMI), help you locate local services to navigate mental health care better.

Schools can also offer critical support. Many have counselors and psychologists who work with students and their families to address mental health concerns. By collaborating with these professionals, you can ensure your teen receives any necessary accommodations or adjustments in their school environment. Teachers are also valuable allies in promoting your teen's well-being. Informing them about your teen's needs helps build a more inclusive and supportive classroom setting.

Community awareness groups, such as Autism Speaks, provide advocacy opportunities and insights to help you better understand and manage your teen's mental health challenges. When you engage with these organizations, you build a robust support system for your teen. Whether through local resources, school services, or awareness groups, this network strengthens your ability to support your teen's mental health.

Peer support programs are another powerful tool for helping your teen connect with others who share similar experiences. These programs, available through schools, community centers, or online platforms, can reduce feelings of isolation and promote a sense of belonging. Peer interactions offer emotional support and practical strategies for managing mental health, making it easier for your teen to relate and feel understood.

Now that we have covered mental health, let us discuss promoting healthy lifestyle habits. These daily routines can impact psychological and physical well-being, supporting your teen's overall health.

Promoting Healthy Lifestyle Habits

It is essential to support autistic teenagers in making and sticking to healthy lifestyle choices for their overall well-being. As a parent or caregiver, you play a crucial role in helping your teen develop practical habits that will serve them as they transition to adulthood. Here are some strategies that help guide your teen toward making healthier choices.

Establishing a Balanced Diet

A balanced diet helps regulate mood and improves cognitive function, both vital for your teen's independence. Introduce a mix of lean proteins, vegetables, fruits, whole grains, and nutritious fats such as seeds and nuts into their diet. Have patience. Autistic teens may need numerous tries before they eat new foods. Nutrient-rich options, like those suggested by the Dietary Guidelines for Americans, can help reduce the risk of chronic diseases.

Meal planning can be a valuable teaching tool. Take these opportunities to talk about how various foods influence their energy and mood. For instance, explain that whole grains offer steady energy, while sugary snacks lead to quick spikes followed by crashes. Reinforce healthy choices with positive feedback, like saying, "Great choice! That snack is fueling your body." Involving your teen in meal prep gives them more control over their diet and helps foster healthy eating habits.

Incorporating Regular Physical Activity

Physical activity is vital for both physical and emotional health. Exercise helps your teen manage stress, boost mood, and regulate emotions. Choose activities they enjoy, like walking, biking, or dancing, so staying active feels fun instead of a task. Encourage them to aim for at least an hour of medium to energetic workout most days.

Incorporate physical activity into your family's routine to set an example. Make exercise fun by planning family outings like hiking or playing soccer so it feels less like a chore. Positive reinforcement like, "You are doing great! Look how fast you are running!" can motivate them to keep going. Structured schedules, with calendars or apps, help maintain consistency. Pairing exercise with something they enjoy, like music, can make it more appealing.

Establishing Sleep Hygiene Practices

Your teen needs 8-10 hours of sleep each night for better cognitive function and emotional regulation. Set a consistent sleep schedule and include calming activities like reading or listening to soft music in their bedtime routine. Reducing screen time before bed helps since blue light from electronics hinders melatonin production.

Ensure their sleep environment is peaceful, unlit, and restful. White noise machines or fans can block distracting sounds, and relaxation techniques like deep breathing can help them unwind. Encourage physical activity to improve sleep quality during the day, but schedule it earlier to avoid interfering with bedtime.

Fostering Independence in Self-Care

Encouraging independence in self-care builds confidence and essential life skills. Start by teaching basic hygiene habits like brushing teeth and grooming. Visual schedules or checklists can help your teen take ownership of these tasks. Slowly augment their duties as they become more confident. Praise their progress to motivate them with positive reinforcement, such as "Great job keeping up with your self-care routine!"

Explain why self-care is essential. Understanding its impact on health and social interactions can motivate teens to stick with these routines. Letting your teen choose their grooming products can make the experience more enjoyable and foster independence.

Beyond hygiene, teach them how to manage personal spaces, like keeping their room tidy and organizing their belongings. These tasks help them gain independence and prepare for adulthood. You can guide them through the process and then gradually step back as they become more confident.

As you focus on building these healthy habits, remember another critical element: managing medications and therapies.

Managing Medications and Therapies

As autistic teenagers transition into adulthood, managing their health becomes a priority. One key aspect of this transition is guiding them through managing medications and therapeutic interventions. It is not just about handing over a pill bottle; it is about helping your teen understand their medication, take responsibility for their health, and develop self-advocacy skills.

Start with open, honest conversations about their medications. Describe the intent of each drug, how it benefits them, and any possible side effects. Use clear, simple language, visual aids, or written explanations if that helps them better understand. When your teen knows why they are taking certain medications, they are more likely to follow through with their treatment. Encourage questions, no matter how basic or complex. Giving honest answers builds trust and helps your teen feel more in control of their health, which improves their cooperation with their medication schedule.

Using visuals like charts or apps to remind them when to take their meds can be a great way to foster independence. When you teach them to manage their medications, they acquire the necessary aptitudes for adulthood. It is about making health management less of a burden and more of a critical part of their well-being.

Therapies also play a significant role in your teen's health. Many autistic teenagers participate in various therapies, including occupational, speech, and behavioral therapy. Keeping all these therapies coordinated can feel overwhelming, but open communication with each therapist makes a huge difference. Regular meetings or updates ensure everyone works toward the same goals, preventing overlapping efforts or overwhelming your teen with disjointed therapy sessions. For instance, if your teen is working on social skills in behavioral therapy, their speech therapist can support that by incorporating similar goals. Creating a unified approach helps your teen progress smoothly without confusion.

Follow-ups are also critical for successful health management. Regular check-ins with healthcare providers and therapists give you a clear picture of how medications and therapies are working. These meetings help you track progress and address issues early before they turn into health crises. Schedule regular reviews of medication effectiveness, side effects, and overall therapeutic progress. A journal can help you track behavior, mood, or health changes. This knowledge allows you to make educated decisions about treatment plans. Sharing these insights with healthcare professionals helps ensure your teen is receiving the best care.

Medication changes can be tricky, especially as your teen grows. You may need to adjust due to side effects or evolving health needs. Stay vigilant when starting or changing a medication; even minor adjustments can cause unexpected reactions. Contact your doctor instantly if you detect shifts in behavior or new symptoms. Staying proactive allows you to handle problems early and stop them from worsening. Having a backup plan, such as alternative therapies or coping strategies, is also helpful if medications need to be paused or changed.

It is important to remember that medication management is not the only part of your teen's health. A holistic approach, including lifestyle changes, can significantly improve their well-being. A balanced diet, routine exercise, and good sleep hygiene are just as essential as medications for non-pharmacological interventions. Encouraging healthy habits can improve your teen's mental and physical health and enhance the effectiveness of their treatments. For example, studies have shown that regular physical activity boosts mood and cognitive function, which can improve the benefits of medications for conditions such as anxiety or ADHD (Holmes, 2022).

As your teen grows, you will want to encourage independence in managing their health. Teaching them to organize their medication schedules, set reminders, and recognize when they need help will build their confidence. Tools like smartphone apps or pill organizers can make this process easier and help your teen feel more in control. They must gradually assume more responsibility to ensure they are ready for adulthood.

In the end, managing medications and therapies is a team effort. With your guidance, you can equip your teen to handle their health as they transition into adulthood, ensuring they have the support needed for a healthy future.

Key Takeaways

- Regular medical checkups help track developmental progress and manage health concerns for autistic teens.

- Health screenings and vaccinations prevent chronic conditions and protect vulnerable immune systems.

- Visual aids and schedules reduce anxiety for autistic teens during medical appointments.

- Mental health support is critical, with early recognition of behavior changes leading to timely intervention.

- Therapists familiar with autism can tailor treatments to individual needs, like cognitive behavioral therapy or social skills training.

- Community resources and peer support groups offer emotional and social connections for teens and families.

- A balanced diet and regular physical activity directly support mental and physical health.

- Sleep hygiene practices, such as consistent schedules and relaxing routines, are essential for emotional regulation.

- Managing medications involves teaching teens to understand their treatments and take responsibility for their health.

As your teen approaches adulthood, another critical aspect of their journey comes into focus—legal considerations. From guardianship to healthcare decision-making, understanding the legal landscape protects your teen's rights and needs. Let us look at the essential steps for confidently navigating these legal responsibilities.

Chapter 7:

Navigating the Legal Landscape

You sit in a crowded lawyer's office, struggling to understand legal terms that seem more like a foreign language than a way to protect your autistic teen. You start questioning whether a law degree is necessary to navigate this labyrinth. The lawyer asks about future planning, and you hesitate. Is this necessary? Then it hits you—yes, it is essential. You are not just dealing with paperwork; you are creating a safety net to ensure your teen's future needs are met long after high school.

Another critical step in planning is understanding guardianship and decision-making for your teen. Let us examine these essential aspects.

Guardianship and Decision-Making

Guardianship and decision-making become crucial as autistic teens near adulthood, bringing new challenges that require thoughtful planning. Once your teen turns 18, the law recognizes them as adults, and you no longer have automatic authority to decide for them. Many autistic teens, particularly those with communication or cognitive difficulties, may struggle with significant decisions, making guardianship a critical solution.

Understanding Guardianship Options

In guardianship, a court designates a guardian to decide for someone who cannot address needs independently. The level of responsibility varies with different types of guardianship. Limited guardianship allows the individual to retain independence in certain areas while receiving support in others. Plenary guardianship gives the guardian complete authority over medical, financial, and decisions.

Before moving forward with guardianship, less restrictive options like the power of attorney or supported decision-making agreements are worth considering. Supported decision-making allows your teen to maintain their legal rights while getting assistance from trusted individuals to help with decisions. This option can be incredibly empowering, promoting independence and aligning with what many self-advocates for autistic people believe—that autonomy is crucial.

Legal Competence and Rights

Deciding whether someone is legally competent is both a sensitive and complicated process. The court must determine that the individual cannot manage specific areas of their life before granting guardianship. This decision involves evaluations by medical professionals and often includes input from educators, caregivers, and others familiar with the individual's abilities.

Some argue that guardianship can be too restrictive, especially in cases where the individual might be capable of making decisions with the right tools and support. The idea that we should always presume competence unless proven otherwise is vital. However, it is also a reality that some autistic teens will need a guardian to ensure their safety and well-being, especially if they have significant intellectual impairments or other challenges that make independent decision-making difficult.

Transitioning Responsibilities

Once the court grants guardianship, the guardian assumes ongoing responsibilities. These include regular reporting to the court and yearly reviews to ensure that the arrangement still serves the individual's best interests. The court conducts these reviews to hold the guardian accountable and ensure they meet the teen's needs as the teen continues to grow and develop.

It is necessary to recognize that guardianship does not have to last forever. Your teen may develop new skills and abilities over time, allowing them to handle more responsibilities. However, changes in the guardian's ability to fulfill their duties or concerns about abuse or neglect could result in modifying or ending the guardianship.

Resources for Legal Counsel

Navigating guardianship can feel overwhelming, but working with a disability law attorney makes a big difference. They will guide you through the legal steps, from gathering evidence to the guardianship hearing, ensuring you are prepared. Beyond legal help, support groups and advocacy organizations offer resources to ease this emotional process. Remember, guardianship impacts your relationship with your teen. Involve them as much as possible, respecting their voice and balancing independence with safety. Guardianship is just one piece of the puzzle, so take time to explore all options, ensuring your teen has the support they need as they transition into adulthood.

Now that you understand the guardianship process, considering what benefits and services might help support your teen's needs is worth considering. From financial assistance to access to specialized services, there is a whole range of resources to help your family. Let us look at the options for disability benefits and services that could make a big difference in your teen's life.

Disability Benefits and Services

Navigating the legal landscape for autistic teenagers as they approach adulthood can feel overwhelming. Understanding the range of disability benefits and services available during this critical transition is essential. Knowing how to access resources can significantly benefit both you and your teen.

Overview of Disability Benefits

When your autistic teen turns 18, they can qualify for substantial federal and state benefits that offer essential support (Graham, n.d.). These benefits typically include Supplemental Security Income (SSI), Medicaid, and Social Security Disability Insurance (SSDI). SSI helps cover basic needs like housing and food. Once they reach 18, your income as a parent no longer affects their eligibility, which can create new opportunities.

SSDI provides support if you or your teen have a work history. The benefit depends on the recipient's or their parents' work history. It is beneficial when a parent has worked and contributed to Social Security.

Medicaid is crucial for health coverage, allowing access to medical care, therapies, and other health services. SSI recipients automatically qualify for Medicaid in many states, but confirming this for your location is essential. Each state administers these programs differently, so staying informed about your state's rules is necessary. Consulting a benefits specialist can also help ensure you maximize available resources.

Accessing Local Services

Local services and federal benefits also play vital roles in helping autistic teens transition to adulthood. The Association of University Centers on Disabilities (AUCD) offers valuable resources for creating transition plans and actively guides families during this critical time.

Local non-profits can also offer valuable assistance. For example, Easterseals provides in-home care, adult day services, employment support, and recreational activities. Their employment services, including job coaching and placement support, can help your teen secure and maintain meaningful employment.

Many states also offer vocational rehabilitation services, training, education, and employment assistance. Engaging with these agencies early can ease your teen's transition into adulthood by ensuring the necessary supports are in place.

The Role of Advocacy Groups

Advocacy groups provide valuable guidance to families during the transition process. Autism Speaks, for example, offers resources and tool kits that simplify the shift to adulthood for autistic teens. These resources include support for individualized education programs (IEPs), post-secondary education, and employment options, empowering you and your teen to make informed choices.

Got Transition focuses on the shift from pediatric to adult healthcare services, offering evidence-based strategies to ensure your teen receives comprehensive care as they grow into adulthood. Preparing for these changes can foster your teen's independence in managing their health.

Long-Term Planning for Benefits

Long-term planning needs frequent assessments and adjustments over time. Knowing how long specific benefits last and when to apply is essential. You should submit SSI and Medicaid applications before your teen turns 18, although the benefits typically start in adulthood (*Transition-Age Youth*, 2018). Register your teen for long-term support services, including housing programs or Medicaid waivers, to ensure they receive the assistance they need.

Legal aspects are also crucial in long-term planning. Turning 18 marks the beginning of legal adulthood, and some autistic teens may need additional support managing personal, financial, or medical decisions. Establishing power of attorney allows you to continue making decisions for your teen. At the same time, guardianship might be necessary for more intensive support. You must evaluate your teen's independence and decide which option fits your family's unique circumstances.

Financial planning is another crucial part of long-term preparation. Opening a special needs trust account can protect your teen's assets without affecting their eligibility for means-tested benefits like SSI and Medicaid. You can use these trusts to pay for services that government programs do not cover, ensuring a higher quality of life for your teen.

Employment is a significant focus area in preparing your teen for adulthood. Organizations like the PACER Center and OCALI offer resources on employment readiness, job matching, and workplace accommodations for individuals with disabilities. These programs emphasize the importance of helping your teen prepare for the workforce or explore appropriate post-secondary educational opportunities.

Encouraging self-advocacy is an essential step in fostering independence in your teen. Teaching them to understand and communicate their needs in various settings, such as school, healthcare, or work, can smooth their transition to adulthood. Life skills workshops and courses can help your teen build the confidence and ability to navigate the world successfully.

As you help your teen prepare for adulthood, you will encounter legal considerations directly affecting their education and employment. Let us now look at how understanding these rights can support your teen in both settings.

Legal Rights in Education and Employment

Understanding the legal rights of autistic teens in educational and workplace environments is vital to helping you advocate for the support, accommodations, and opportunities your teen needs to thrive. Navigating these legal frameworks ensures your teen receives the resources and protection they deserve as they transition into adulthood.

Educational Rights: IDEA and ADA

The Individuals with Disabilities Education Act (IDEA) and the Americans with Disabilities Act (ADA) are crucial in protecting autistic teens. These laws guarantee that teens receive equal access to education and the necessary accommodations to address their specific needs.

Individuals With Disabilities Education Act (IDEA)

Under IDEA, public schools must develop an Individualized Education Plan (IEP) for every student with a disability, including autistic teens. The IEP outlines your teen's specific educational goals and details the services they will receive, such as specialized instruction, speech and language therapy, occupational therapy, or behavioral support. This individualized approach helps your teen actively engage in their education.

Americans With Disabilities Act (ADA)

The ADA protects students with disabilities in K-12 education, higher education, and public services. Schools, colleges, and universities must offer reasonable accommodations to ensure equal educational opportunities. Accommodations such as extended test time, note-taking assistance, and assistive technology help autistic teens perform at their best.

Transition Services in Education

As your teen approaches graduation, transition services become essential to their education. These services prepare your teen for life after high school, whether heading to further education, entering the workforce, or aiming for independent living. Ideally, transition planning should begin at 16 but can start earlier if needed.

Critical elements of effective transition planning include:

- **Career Exploration and Training:** Schools should give autistic teens opportunities to explore different career paths and develop job skills. This might involve internships, vocational training, work-study programs, or job coaching tailored to their interests and strengths.
- **Independent Living Skills:** Teaching your teen practical life skills, like managing finances, cooking, and self-care, will boost

their confidence. These essential abilities help them transition into adulthood with greater ease.

- **Support for Post-Secondary Education:** If your teen plans to pursue higher education, it is vital to include information on support services available at colleges and universities. Disability resource centers often provide academic accommodations and counseling, helping students succeed in the next chapter of their lives.

As a parent or caregiver, you play a vital part in your teen's transition process. Collaborating with the school and professionals ensures your teen's goals stay realistic and achievable. Advocating for your teen is crucial in developing a thorough and effective transition plan.

Legal Protections in Employment

Stepping into the workplace presents new challenges for autistic teens, but understanding the legal protections in place helps ensure they are treated fairly and given equal opportunities.

Prohibition of Discrimination

The ADA ensures that employers cannot discriminate against individuals with disabilities, including autistic teens, in hiring, promotions, job assignments, and training. They must offer equal opportunities and evaluate your teen based on their abilities and qualifications, not their disability.

Reasonable Accommodations in the Workplace

Employers are required to provide reasonable accommodations that enable employees with autism to perform their job duties effectively. Examples of these accommodations include:

- **Flexible Work Hours:** Adjusting work schedules can accommodate sensory overload or fatigue, giving your teen the support they need to thrive.

- **Quiet Workspaces:** A designated quiet area can minimize distractions and create a more comfortable environment for your teen to stay focused.

- **Visual Aids:** Using visual instructions, schedules, or task reminders can help your teen stay organized and manage tasks more effectively.

- **Technology Adaptations:** Implementing specialized software or tools tailored to your teen's needs can boost job performance and accessibility.

Employers must consider accommodation requests and work with employees to find fair and practical solutions. Open communication between employers and employees is essential to ensure accommodations are tailored to individual needs while maintaining workplace efficiency.

Resolving Disputes

When disagreements arise over educational or workplace accommodations, knowing how to resolve these issues effectively is essential.

Education-Related Disputes

Suppose you believe the school is not addressing your teen's educational needs. In that case, you can request a meeting to raise your concerns and discuss revising their IEP. If the problem persists, IDEA allows you to pursue mediation or a due process hearing to resolve the dispute effectively.

Workplace-Related Disputes

If your teen faces discrimination or their accommodation needs are not met, they can file a complaint with the Equal Employment Opportunity Commission (EEOC). The EEOC investigates the claims and takes appropriate action to guarantee fair treatment.

Understanding these dispute resolution processes can help you protect your teen's rights and ensure they receive the support they deserve in school and the workplace.

With educational and employment rights in hand, you are helping your teen move toward a brighter future. Next, let us focus on an essential aspect of growing up—transitioning out of pediatric care and into adult healthcare services. It is a significant milestone for your teen and one you will want to approach with care and planning.

Transitioning Out of Pediatric Care

Navigating the transition from pediatric to adult healthcare can feel overwhelming for parents, caregivers, and professionals supporting autistic teenagers. This phase comes with challenges like understanding new healthcare needs, finding appropriate providers, and fostering independence in young adults. To manage this process effectively, you must grasp the transition steps, create solid healthcare plans, involve your teen in decisions, and utilize available resources.

Understanding the Transition Process

Transitioning from pediatric to adult healthcare happens gradually and requires thorough planning. In pediatric care, parents typically take a central role in making decisions. Adult care focuses on the individual, expecting them to manage their health. However, according to a 2018 American Academy of Family Physicians (AAFP) report, only 15% of youth receive transition planning support from healthcare professionals (*Updated Clinical Report*, 2018). This gap highlights the importance of a structured approach to ensuring autistic teens receive uninterrupted care.

The *Six Core Elements of Health Care Transition*, created by Got Transition/Center for Health Care Transition Improvement, offers a helpful framework for this process. It emphasizes establishing clear policies, tracking progress, building self-care skills, and ensuring a seamless transfer to adult care. With this model, you and your teen can effectively prepare for the transition into adult healthcare.

Creating Healthcare Plans

Creating a comprehensive healthcare plan is critical to a smooth transition. Begin by talking with your teen's pediatrician to understand their specific needs, including any required specialties for adult care. Review medications, therapies, and ongoing treatments, and document everything to share it easily with new providers.

You will want to understand how pediatric healthcare differs from adult care. Pediatric care typically includes specialists working together, while adult care often expects your teen to manage appointments independently. Help your teen take on this responsibility by tracking their medical history, setting appointment reminders, and managing their medications effectively.

Involvement in Healthcare Decisions

Empowering your teen to participate in healthcare decisions is vital to fostering independence. This involvement helps them become more comfortable in adult healthcare settings. Start by including them in discussions with their healthcare providers and encourage them to voice their concerns and preferences. This builds their confidence and ensures they understand their health and treatment options.

Teaching self-advocacy skills is also essential. These skills help teens communicate effectively with healthcare professionals, ask important questions, and make informed decisions about their care. You can practice these scenarios by role-playing conversations with doctors or nurses. You should also provide resources like books or online materials to help teens understand their health and navigate the healthcare system.

Resources for Adult Health Care

Finding healthcare providers experienced with autistic teenagers is vital. Not all professionals have the necessary expertise, so seeking those who do is essential. Ask your teen's pediatrician to recommend adult healthcare providers familiar with autism. You can also contact support groups and advocacy organizations to locate suitable providers.

In addition to medical professionals, look into community resources that support autistic adults. Many communities offer programs for counseling, job training, social skills workshops, and other services that can help during the transition to adulthood. Also, remember to consider the financial aspects of health care. As your teen moves to adult care, there may be changes in insurance coverage or eligibility for government programs. Be sure to review these changes to maintain access to necessary services.

By thoughtfully preparing for this transition, you can help your autistic teenager smoothly move into the adult healthcare system, promoting both their health and independence.

Key Takeaways

- Guardianship may be necessary once your teen turns 18. Still, consider less restrictive options like power of attorney or supported decision-making first.

- Guardianship requires regular reviews to ensure it continues to serve the teen's best interests and can be adjusted as circumstances change.

- Disability law attorneys and advocacy organizations can provide valuable support in navigating guardianship and decision-making processes.

- Local services, including vocational rehabilitation and job coaching, assist autistic teens in securing employment and gaining independence.

- Long-term planning should include applying for benefits, establishing guardianship or power of attorney, and setting up a special needs trust.

- The ADA requires employers to offer reasonable accommodations, such as flexible work hours or quiet spaces, to support autistic employees.

- Transition planning for autistic teens includes career exploration, independent living skills, and support for post-secondary education.

- Transitioning from pediatric to adult health care requires a structured plan, empowering autistic teens to manage their health independently.

As your autistic teen moves into adulthood, a strong support network is essential. Legal and financial planning matter, but connecting your teen with the right people and resources ensures they receive the guidance and emotional support needed to succeed. Let us look at how to create this critical network.

Chapter 8:

Building a Support Network

One morning, you decided to brave the wilds of a PTA meeting. Armed with coffee and optimism, you mentioned needing a support network for your autistic teen. Immediately, three parents chimed in with their own stories, and suddenly, you were not alone. Between sharing resources and those knowing nods of understanding, you realize that sometimes the best support comes from people who have already walked your path. By the end, you felt a little lighter, and your coffee? Still cold, but it was worth it.

Next, consider joining advocacy groups to share your voice and ensure support for your teen's future.

Forming Connections With Advocacy Groups

Connecting with advocacy groups that specialize in supporting autistic individuals and their families can be an invaluable resource for parents. These organizations offer a wealth of tools and guidance to help you navigate significant life transitions for your teen, whether moving from school to work or transitioning into adulthood. Their support ensures you are well-prepared to assist your teen through these changes.

Understanding Available Resources

One of the most significant advantages of joining advocacy groups is the access to critical resources that simplify the transition process.

These groups provide clear, practical guides to help you navigate complex systems like health care and education.

For example, many advocacy groups offer insights into laws like the Autism CARES Act, which affects health care and educational services for autistic individuals. This legislation ensures that crucial support programs and resources remain accessible to families like yours. Staying informed about such legislation is essential because it directly impacts the services available to your teen.

These organizations also help you manage the often confusing bureaucratic processes. They can assist you in securing an Individualized Education Plan (IEP), arranging therapy sessions, or finding job training programs. Access to this information enables you to support your teen better as they work toward greater independence. Advocacy groups ensure you receive the necessary services when you need them most.

Networking With Peers

Advocacy groups also offer a priceless benefit to the community. Linking with other households who share similar backgrounds offers comfort and empowerment. You are not alone in raising an autistic teenager, and talking to other parents who truly understand can help lighten your emotional load.

You can participate in support meetings, online forums, or regular meet-ups through these groups. These spaces allow you to share your journey, exchange tips, and recommend local service providers. For instance, you might connect with another parent who has found an excellent occupational therapist, or perhaps you will be the one offering advice on managing school transitions.

Research supports the value of peer support. A study in the Journal of Autism and Developmental Disorders found that parents who engage with peer groups experience lower stress levels and greater emotional resilience (Drogomyretska et al., 2020). Sharing your challenges and successes with others creates a strong emotional and practical support network that can make the journey easier for everyone involved.

Staying Informed on Legislation

Another crucial function of advocacy groups is updating you on legislative changes affecting autism services. Laws can change quickly, and staying informed is vital to ensure your teen receives the full range of available benefits. Advocacy groups often send newsletters, host webinars, and organize informational sessions to keep you in the loop.

For example, changes to laws like the Autism CARES Act or the Individuals with Disabilities Education Act (IDEA) can directly impact the support services available to your teen. Advocacy groups are often the first to inform families of these changes and help explain how they might affect your family. Being informed lets you act quickly when necessary, ensuring your teen does not miss out on meaningful opportunities.

Involvement in advocacy efforts can also be fulfilling. Many parents find a sense of purpose in supporting legislative campaigns that benefit their children. Your participation ensures that future generations of autistic teens can continue to access critical resources and services.

Access to Training Events

Advocacy groups do not just provide information—they offer workshops and training sessions that help you and your teen develop crucial skills for the future. These events, often led by experts, give you access to the latest research-based strategies to help your family manage day-to-day challenges and plan for the future.

Workshops for teens may focus on skills like communication, social interaction, and job readiness. For instance, a teen may attend a session on handling job interviews or navigating social cues in the workplace. On the other hand, parents may benefit from workshops on effective advocacy techniques, understanding autism more intensely, or supporting their teen's transition into adulthood.

A great example of this is workshops that focus on creating personalized transition plans, helping teens map out their journey from high school to adult life. These plans can include goals like employment, further education, or independent living. Research shows that autistic teens who engage in job training programs are likelier to find employment as adults (Weiss & LeBlanc, 2019).

Training events also allow you to ask professionals specific questions about your situation. Whether you are unsure how to start the transition process or need advice on a particular challenge, these sessions provide expert guidance tailored to your needs.

Engaging with advocacy groups is about more than finding resources—building a supportive community. These organizations offer practical advice, connect you with other families, and inform you about crucial legislative changes. They also provide opportunities for you and your teen to develop the skills to transition into adulthood.

Now that you have built connections within the broader autism community, it is time to bring extended family members into the conversation. Expanding your teen's support network is critical in helping them thrive. Let us look at how you can get your family involved.

Engaging Extended Family Members

Involving extended family members in your support network can significantly impact your autistic teen's development and transition to adulthood. When family members understand and show empathy, they build a supportive environment that strengthens your teen's growth and independence. Research emphasizes that educating the extended family about autism is critical (*10 Ways*, 2023). When relatives understand autism's characteristics—like challenges with social interactions or sensory sensitivities—they are better prepared to provide meaningful support.

A practical way to begin is by offering them resources—articles, books, or even inviting them to participate in therapy sessions. For instance, explaining how your teen might need a quiet space after feeling overwhelmed can help relatives adjust their expectations. Communication should be ongoing, encouraging open discussion and addressing family members' questions. This keeps everyone aligned and strengthens the support system.

Workshops or informal family gatherings with health professionals are another effective strategy. Such events can debunk misconceptions about autism while personalizing the experience, helping your relatives understand your teen's needs and strengths. Encouraging consistency and routine, which are vital for autistic teens, can further ease family involvement. Routines offer your teen comfort and security, so letting family members know what works best for your household will make a huge difference.

Creating an extended network of support allows more people to assist when necessary. Whether it is a grandparent offering after-school care or an uncle helping with transportation to appointments, spreading responsibilities ensures that your teen has multiple sources of support during transitions or stressful times. Assigning roles based on individual strengths is also crucial. For example, if an aunt excels at planning, she could organize social activities, which can be fun and an opportunity for your teen to practice essential life skills.

Participating in family events helps your teen build independence. Extended family members can serve as role models or companions during outings, whether joining a local hobby group or simply spending time together on everyday tasks like cooking. These interactions help your teen feel a sense of belonging and boost their confidence, which are crucial as they move toward adulthood.

Celebrating milestones with extended family strengthens positive reinforcement. Whether through verbal praise, a high-five, or a family dinner to recognize a new accomplishment, these moments raise your teen's self-esteem. Keeping everyone updated with group messages or social media ensures the family stays involved and engaged in your teen's growth. You could also set up an "achievement board" to showcase successes, offering a visual reminder of your teen's progress.

Inviting family members to participate in these moments strengthens the family bond. It demonstrates to your teen that their efforts are seen and valued. Gratitude goes both ways. Acknowledging the contributions of extended family—whether through thank-you notes or simple verbal recognition—keeps the support system strong and engaged.

Next, let us consider how community programs can play a crucial role in continuing this support and fostering further connections for your teen's development. These programs offer structured opportunities to build independence and social skills while involving your teen in the broader community.

Utilizing Community Programs

When your autistic teen starts transitioning into adulthood, it can feel like you are navigating uncharted waters. One of the most significant steps in easing this transition is understanding the local programs and resources available. Communities often have programs specifically designed for teens with disabilities. Still, they can be tricky to find if you do not know where to look. These programs range from educational initiatives to social support networks, all tailored to make this transition smoother.

Start by looking into the institutions available in your area. Many offer support services like individualized plans, therapies, and family counseling. For example, local and regional centers or developmental service departments can be great starting points. In California, for instance, the Department of Developmental Services offers the "Transition to Adulthood" program, which helps families of teens with disabilities navigate this period of life. Parents should contact these organizations directly, ask about available services, and clarify eligibility requirements.

Online directories like those provided by Autism Speaks, or state disability resources can be invaluable in finding programs close to home. Government offices, such as city hall or local health departments, are also great places to contact. However, one of the most reliable ways to discover what's available is to network with other parents in your community. Other parents have likely experienced the same challenges and can provide insight into programs they have found effective.

The Value of Social Skills Groups

One of the most beneficial community programs for autistic teens is social skills groups. Trained professionals lead these groups, creating structured environments where teens can actively practice social interactions. Knowing that their teen has a safe space to learn social cues and communication strategies can bring immense relief for many parents.

In these groups, teens practice conversation starters, learn how to maintain eye contact, and even pick up nonverbal cues like body language. Research shows that autistic teens who join social skills groups often experience significant improvement in their ability to handle social situations. For example, a study by the Journal of Autism and Developmental Disorders found that teens participating in social skills programs showed improved peer interactions and reduced social anxiety (Parenteau et al., 2024).

Role-playing exercises are often used in these groups to simulate real-life social situations. Teens practice handling common social challenges like joining a conversation or recognizing when it is their turn to speak. Some programs also include group discussions that encourage open dialogue about the difficulties they face in social situations.

If you are looking for these programs, start with local non-profits, therapy clinics, or educational institutions. Autism-focused organizations such as the Autism Society or local community centers often list available social skills programs. It is also a good idea to visit a session or two before signing up to ensure the atmosphere and teaching style are a good fit for your teen. You want a program that feels encouraging and manageable.

Job Readiness Programs: Preparing for Independence

Job readiness programs are another vital resource for autistic teens as they approach adulthood. These programs combine skills training with real-world experiences to help teens become more independent. They typically offer a mix of workshops, internships, and career counseling to prepare participants for the workforce.

The primary focus often centers on soft skills like communication, teamwork, and problem-solving. For instance, some programs teach how to handle feedback from a supervisor or navigate workplace dynamics. Hard skills—job-specific—might include tasks like data entry, cooking, or customer service, depending on the career path.

Many communities partner with local businesses to create internship opportunities. These internships are often a teen's first experience in a work environment, allowing them to develop hands-on skills while gaining confidence. The Autism Society's Employment Programs, for example, help match autistic teens to internships that suit their abilities and interests. These real-world experiences develop job-related skills and boost independence and self-esteem.

One example of success is the Microsoft Autism Hiring Program, which provides teens and young adults with autism a supportive environment to learn coding and other tech skills. These programs show that when autistic teens have the right resources, they can succeed in the workplace.

Parents can encourage teens to start job readiness programs early to maximize the benefits. Checking in with schools, vocational training centers, or local employment agencies can give you a good lead on available programs. Additionally, look out for opportunities like mock interviews or resume-building workshops—critical tools for job seekers.

Getting Involved in Sports and Recreation Activities

Participating in sports and recreation activities is not just about staying fit; it is also a chance for your teen to build essential social and team skills. Community programs often offer inclusive sports leagues and recreational activities that cater to individuals with disabilities, providing a welcoming environment where teens can thrive.

Physical activities have numerous benefits, from improving health to boosting social confidence. For autistic teens, structured physical activities like swimming, yoga, or dance can be both fun and therapeutic. Studies show that regular physical activity improves physical health and mental well-being, with participants showing reduced anxiety levels and improved mood.

Teens learn critical life skills like working as part of a team, following rules and handling competition. For instance, inclusive soccer or basketball leagues, often organized by groups like Special Olympics, provide structured environments where teens can enjoy camaraderie. Coaches should have experience with autistic teens to create supportive and successful experiences.

Many local YMCAs, parks, recreation departments, and specialized community centers offer these programs. Parents should research and visit facilities to confirm that staff members receive sufficient training and that the environment suits their teens.

Maximizing Community Resources for a Smooth Transition

Once you have found the right programs, knowing how to use them effectively can significantly impact your teen's transition to adulthood. Consider these practical steps:

1. **Research Thoroughly:** Take your time investigating all available programs in your community. You can gather

information effectively through online directories, community bulletin boards, and word-of-mouth.

2. **Visit Programs:** Before committing, visit a few programs to ensure they align with your teen's needs and interests. The environment and staff are crucial to success.

3. **Stay Informed:** Keep checking for updates or new programs that might pop up. Resources can change yearly, so staying in the loop ensures you know the latest opportunities.

4. **Encourage Consistency:** Encourage regular attendance, as consistent participation leads to better outcomes. Programs are most effective when they become a consistent part of your teen's routine.

5. **Communicate With Providers:** Maintain open communication with program staff. Your feedback can help tailor activities to suit your teen's needs better.

6. **Involve Your Teen:** Let them vote on which programs they want to join. Keeping them enthusiastic and engaged greatly boosts their chances of success.

Next, we will focus on how you can communicate effectively with your support team, ensuring that everyone works together to help your teen succeed.

Effective Communication With the Support Team

Creating effective communication between parents, educators, and support teams is essential when supporting autistic teenagers. Clear and consistent communication ensures everyone works toward shared goals, tailoring strategies to meet the teen's needs. As a parent, you have invaluable knowledge about your teen's behaviors and needs, making you an essential part of the team. When you share insights, like how your teen might experience sensory overload, educators and therapists can adapt their approaches, whether adjusting classroom environments or modifying teaching methods.

This information exchange does not stop with parents. Educators and support staff should also provide updates, like progress reports and observations on what strategies work in the classroom. For example, suppose a particular focus method helps in school. In that case, you can implement a similar approach at home, creating consistency for your teen. Building this consistent routine can make a significant difference, as studies have shown that parental involvement in a child's education leads to improved academic and social outcomes.

Collaboration plays a vital role. When parents, teachers, and therapists share their unique perspectives, they create more effective strategies. Parents' insights into daily routines, educators' observations of social interactions, and therapists' targeted interventions all help develop a balanced support plan. Holding regular, structured meetings ensures every team member can discuss successes and concerns, allowing strategies to be adjusted accordingly.

Feedback is vital in refining these strategies. It should be a two-way street, with all parties observing and reporting how interventions work. For instance, if a new method helps reduce your teen's anxiety, feedback from you, the educators, and the therapists will help fine-tune the approach. Regular feedback and open dialogue are critical, especially when things are unplanned. Addressing challenges as they arise allows the team to make adjustments and try new solutions without frustration building up.

Regular communication does not have to be formal. A simple phone call, email, or even a message through an app can keep everyone aligned. Schools increasingly use technology to streamline this communication, from apps that update parents on progress to video calls for quick check-ins. Keeping the lines open builds trust and helps foster stronger relationships among everyone involved.

Incorporating empathy into communication is essential. Acknowledge that educators may balance many students' needs just as you juggle your teen's needs with other responsibilities. Recognizing each other's challenges helps build mutual respect and strengthen collaboration. When everyone feels heard and valued, remaining committed and engaged in your teen's journey is more effortless.

Effective communication benefits the team and directly impacts your teen's development and success. Whether sharing valuable insights, collaboratively crafting action plans, or maintaining consistent dialogue, transparent and open communication creates a cohesive support environment that empowers your teen to thrive as they transition into adulthood.

Key Takeaways

- Effective communication between parents, educators, and support teams is crucial for supporting autistic teenagers.

- Sharing information like sensory triggers helps educators and therapists tailor their strategies.

- Consistent routines, with parental involvement, lead to improved academic and social outcomes for autistic teens.

- Feedback from all parties refines strategies and ensures interventions are effective.

- Empathetic communication builds trust, strengthens collaboration, and respects each party's challenges.

As your teen grows, preparing for the future extends beyond education and daily support. Financial planning becomes essential to ensure their long-term security. The next chapter will cover critical strategies for building a solid financial foundation, including budgeting, saving, and exploring available resources for autistic teens.

Chapter 9:

Financial Planning for the Future

You sit down with your teen, eager to talk about financial planning. Armed with spreadsheets, a budgeting app, and colorful charts, you are ready. Your teen looks at the charts, nods, and asks, "Can we use this money to buy all the Pokémon cards?" You smile, realizing there is work ahead. Although the conversation does not go as planned, this is just the beginning. Step by step, you are guiding your teen to see that financial planning is not just for today; it is about building freedom for the future.

Next, it is time to focus on the here and now—budgeting and managing personal finances. Practical strategies can help your teen make sense of money today.

Budgeting and Managing Personal Finances

Understanding how income and expenses work is essential for autistic teenagers as they build financial literacy. Helping them grasp how money flows in and out will set them up for better financial management. Start by explaining that income can come from different sources, like an allowance, part-time jobs, or gifts. This shows them that money is earned or received, not something that appears magically.

Next, discuss expenses with your teen by explaining where their money goes, such as subscriptions, transportation, or saving for a new gadget. Help them understand the balance between earning and spending by encouraging them to track monthly income and expenses in a notebook or spreadsheet. This practice helps them identify spending patterns and gain control over their financial behavior. As tracking becomes a regular habit, they can adjust their spending based on the insights they gather.

Talking about your finances at home can also help them. Share responsibilities like paying bills or budgeting for groceries. This transparency offers real-life examples, helping them see how money management works and how important it is.

Creating a Budget

Once your teen understands income and expenses, guide them through creating a budget. This plan maps out how to allocate money over a month. Begin by listing their income sources and identifying fixed income, like allowance, and variable income from chores or part-time work, showing them income is not always consistent.

Next, list their expenses by dividing them into essentials like transportation and school supplies and non-essentials like snacks and entertainment. Teaching your teen to prioritize needs over wants will enhance their money management aptitudes. Guide them to allocate funds for necessary expenses first and ensure they do not overspend. If their expenses exceed their income, take the opportunity to discuss how they can reduce costs or increase earnings. Use budget templates or a simple sheet of paper to walk them through the process. Regularly examine the budget to ensure it stays flexible as their needs change.

Developing Saving Habits

The next step after budgeting is to highlight the significance of saving. Starting early helps teens develop this crucial habit. Show your teen the "pay yourself first" approach, where they save a portion of their income before spending on anything else. This reinforces that saving is as significant as paying bills.

Guide your teen to set specific short-term and long-term savings goals. For example, they save for a gadget or concert tickets in the short term, while long-term goals could focus on college or a car. Breaking down these goals helps make saving more manageable. A visual savings chart can motivate them, and tracking progress boosts their confidence.

Consider offering incentives for savings, such as matching a portion of their contributions or celebrating milestones. If they have a savings account, explain how compound interest works so they can see how their money can grow over time. This helps them understand the benefits of patience and planning.

Using Personal Finance Apps

Personal finance apps help make financial literacy more interactive. For autistic teens, who often respond well to visual aids, these apps can simplify money management. One option is GoHenry, a prepaid debit card paired with a financial management app. It allows you to set spending limits while your teen can track their spending and savings in real time. Goodbudget helps organize spending by using virtual envelopes, which show precisely how much money remains in each category.

Encourage your teen to explore various apps and discover the one that best serves their requirements. Guide them through the app's features and explain how to protect their financial information. As they gain confidence, they will increasingly take on the responsibility of managing their finances using these tools.

You equip your autistic teen to achieve financial independence by helping them understand income and expenses, create a budget, develop saving habits, and use finance apps. Each step strengthens their financial literacy, ensuring they have the tools to manage their money responsibly and succeed in the future.

Now that your teen understands budgeting and saving, it is time to consider long-term security. Let us look at savings plans and special needs trusts—crucial tools for ensuring financial stability for the future.

Savings Plans and Special Needs Trusts

Securing financial stability for autistic teens during their transition to adulthood may feel daunting, but it is essential. As a parent or caregiver, you need to protect their future while ensuring they remain eligible for benefits like Supplemental Security Income (SSI) or Medicaid. Thankfully, various savings options allow you to achieve financial stability without risking these critical benefits. Here are some approaches to support securing your teen's economic future.

Types of Savings Plans

Two primary savings tools can help individuals with disabilities: 529 plans and ABLE accounts. Each has distinct advantages; understanding both can help you make informed decisions.

529 Plans

529 plans have traditionally offered tax advantages for educational expenses. Now, you can transfer funds from a 529 plan to an ABLE account for your teen's education without incurring penalties or taxes. This flexibility is helpful if financial priorities change, allowing you to use the funds for broader living expenses if college plans shift.

ABLE Accounts

ABLE (Achieving a Better Life Experience) accounts are specifically designed for individuals with disabilities, allowing families to save up to $18,000 per year without affecting SSI or Medicaid eligibility (*Spotlight*, n.d.). These funds can cover many expenses, from housing and health care to transportation and assistive technology while growing tax-free. This flexibility makes ABLE accounts a fantastic way to support your teen's future without risking essential benefits.

Establishing a Special Needs Trust

A special needs trust (SNT) is vital in securing your teen's economic future while maintaining their eligibility for government help. You can choose between two types of SNTs: first-party and third-party.

First-Party Special Needs Trusts

Your teen's assets, like an inheritance or settlement, fund a first-party trust. These funds will not disqualify your teen from receiving Medicaid or SSI. However, any remaining funds after your teen's passing must reimburse Medicaid for services provided.

Third-Party Special Needs Trusts

Parents or relatives usually fund third-party trusts to benefit the individual. Unlike first-party trusts, Medicaid does not require repayment after your teen passes away. This makes third-party trusts a strong choice for long-term planning.

Funding the Trust

After establishing the trust, you must fund it actively to ensure its effectiveness. Several strategies can provide long-term financial security for your teen.

Direct Contributions

Family and friends can contribute directly to the trust; even small, regular contributions can build a substantial financial foundation over time.

Life Insurance Policies

Parents frequently fund the trust through life insurance policies. The trust receives the proceeds when they pass away, securing their teen's financial future. This method offers reassurance, knowing their teen will have the support they need even in their absence.

Retirement Accounts

You can designate the special needs trust as a beneficiary of your retirement accounts, such as an IRA or 401(k). This allows those funds to support your teen without triggering tax burdens.

Reviewing and Updating Financial Plans

Financial planning is not a one-time task. It is essential to regularly review and update your strategies to ensure they still align with your teen's needs and the changing landscape of government benefits.

Periodic Reviews

Review your financial plans annually to keep your strategies effective as your teen's needs change and benefits laws evolve. Regular reviews help ensure your approach stays aligned with their growth and any regulation updates.

Professional Assistance

Working with attorneys and financial advisors specializing in special needs planning offers invaluable support. They guide you through complex rules and confirm your plans follow legal prerequisites. Their expertise helps you stay prepared for any changes in government policies and make necessary adjustments to protect your teen's future.

Flexibility in Planning

Building flexibility into your financial strategy is essential. Life is unpredictable, and having a plan that adapts to your teen's changing needs or shifts in government benefits ensures that you can adjust without significant disruptions.

Securing your teen's financial future gives you peace of mind, knowing they will have the support they need, no matter what challenges life presents.

Now that you have a solid foundation for long-term financial security, the next step is understanding how to access financial aid and scholarships to further support your teen's journey into adulthood. These resources can open up additional opportunities and provide vital support as your teen takes the next steps toward independence.

Accessing Financial Aid and Scholarships

Finding the right financial aid and scholarships for autistic teens can feel overwhelming at first. Still, with a focused approach, you can guide your teen toward securing the support they need. Your role as a parent involves:

- exploring various financial aid options
- using school and community resources
- helping your teen through the process step by step

The initial stage is understanding the various types of economic aid. You will find grants, scholarships, and loans as crucial options. Grants are based on monetary needs and do not need repayment, making them a great choice. Scholarships, whether merit-based or need-based, also do not need repayment. Scholarships offer financial support and encourage inclusion and long-term success for teens. Loans require repayment with interest and can serve as a backup when other funding sources fall short.

Scholarships designed for autistic teens provide valuable support, covering tuition and expenses like specialized evaluations or college prep programs. These costs can quickly increase, so scholarships become an essential financial resource. You can easily find scholarships that fit your criteria, including disability, using platforms like U.S. News Scholarship Finder, Scholarships.com, College Board's Big Future, and Fastweb. These sites simplify your search for relevant scholarships, making the process much more efficient.

Once you have identified potential scholarships, navigating the application process comes next. Gather necessary documents like proof of disability, academic records, and recommendation letters. Carefully review eligibility requirements and track application deadlines. Many scholarships require an essay, so encourage your teen to write about their personal experiences, goals, and how receiving the scholarship would impact their education. Tailoring each essay to the specific scholarship increases their chances of standing out.

Staying organized helps prevent overwhelm. Encourage your teen to use a calendar to track deadlines and set reminders for each application. This approach minimizes stress and ensures they meet every deadline without last-minute pressure.

Do not overlook the resources available through your teen's school. School counselors often know about financial aid options for autistic students and can guide you through the process. Some schools even have scholarships, particularly for learners with disabilities. Additionally, disability services offices at colleges can help identify internal and external funding opportunities and provide support throughout the application process, improving your teen's chances of securing aid.

Working with school counselors can also strengthen applications. Counselors may recommend highlighting additional expenses, like executive functioning coaches or social skills programs, which are essential for your teen's success but frequently overlooked in typical applications. Highlighting these needs can increase the likelihood of receiving aid that covers such critical services.

You can also find financial aid opportunities by networking within your community. Organizations like Autism Speaks, and the National Autism Association can offer guidance on financial aid and connect you with helpful resources. Contact your state's Developmental Disabilities Council for scholarships specifically for autistic teens. Some states' vocational rehabilitation agencies may offer financial assistance if a college degree is essential for your teen's career path.

Remember to consider community organizations that do not specifically focus on autism. Local groups like Rotary Clubs or faith-based organizations often offer scholarships or funding for local students. These smaller, local scholarships tend to be less competitive, increasing your teen's chances of receiving financial aid. Attending local events or connecting through community centers may uncover additional opportunities.

Successfully navigating the financial aid process requires persistence and knowing where to search. By utilizing school resources, community networks, and a focused scholarship search strategy, you ensure your teen secures the financial support necessary for their education and future. While it takes effort, giving your teen the tools to succeed is worth it.

Now that you have got a handle on financial aid and scholarships, let us move on to another important topic: preparing for independent living expenses. This step is all about helping your teen develop practical money management skills so they can confidently manage their finances in the real world.

Preparing for Independent Living Expenses

When your autistic teen starts thinking about independent living, understanding monthly living costs becomes crucial. You want them to feel confident and prepared, and breaking down everyday expenses will help them manage their budget effectively.

Housing typically takes up the most significant portion of expenses, including rent, utilities like electricity and water, internet, and renter's insurance. In 2024, the average American household spends around $6,440 monthly on various expenses (*The Average*, 2024). Although a single-person household may have lower costs, knowing these figures will help you and your teen plan more effectively for their future.

Food and transportation are also critical parts of a monthly budget. Food costs can fluctuate depending on whether your teen cooks at home or orders takeout. Sometimes meal prepping saves money, but takeout offers convenience. Transportation costs will vary, too, depending on whether they use public transit or have a car. Owning a car involves expenses like insurance, gas, and maintenance, while public transit comes with the cost of monthly passes. These daily expenses need careful attention to avoid going over budget.

Other categories to account for include personal insurance, health care, entertainment, clothing, and everyday items like toiletries and cleaning supplies. By breaking down these costs, you can help your teen see the bigger picture and prepare for all the essentials.

Creating a Realistic Spending Plan

A spending plan is essential for your teen to keep track of their income and expenses. Without one, it is easy to lose control of finances. Introduce your teen to categorizing their income and separating needs from wants.

The 50/30/20 rule offers a straightforward framework. Your teen should use 50 percent of their income to cover necessities like rent, groceries, and utilities. They can allocate 30 percent for discretionary spending, such as entertainment or dining out. In comparison, the remaining 20 percent goes toward savings or debt repayment (Whiteside, 2024). This method helps your teen structure their money management effectively.

Help your teen track their income—whether from a financial aid, allowance, or part-time job—over several months to compare it with their expenses. Use online tools and apps to make the approach more fascinating and effortless. Regularly using these tools will reinforce responsible financial habits for your teen.

Collaborate with your teen throughout this process to make it a joint effort, not a lecture. Ask questions, explore solutions together, and work as a team. Autistic teens are more likely to take ownership and build confidence in managing money when they feel supported and actively involved in decisions.

Exploring Affordable Housing Options

After your autistic teen masters budgeting, the next step is exploring affordable housing options. There are numerous alternatives, each with its benefits and drawbacks. Public housing and government-provided vouchers reduce rent costs, making independent living more affordable. Though these programs may take time to secure, they are valuable resources worth considering.

Shared living arrangements are another option. Sharing rent and utilities with roommates can significantly reduce expenses. Although this requires flexibility and good communication, it is an effective way to cut costs. Help your teen research potential roommates, visit housing options, and find a setup that fits their needs.

Some states offer housing programs designed for individuals with disabilities, providing tailored accommodations and financial support. Community resources and non-profits may also offer grants or assistance for low-income individuals, including those with special needs.

Building an Emergency Fund

Creating an emergency fund is necessary for your teen's economic security. It furnishes a safety net for unexpected costs such as medical bills, car rehabilitation, or a temporary loss of income. This fund offers your teen peace of mind, knowing they have a financial cushion for emergencies.

Experts suggest saving three to six months of living costs. This goal may feel daunting, but reassure your teen that even small, steady savings add up. For instance, putting aside $50 monthly leads to $600 after a year. Explain compound interest to show how their savings can steadily grow, making it more motivating.

Help your teen develop a plan for building their emergency fund, stressing that this money is for true emergencies, not daily expenses. This habit of saving will create long-term financial security and help your teen approach independent living with more confidence.

By teaching your teen essential financial skills, you help them succeed as they move toward independent living. You can work alongside them to navigate budgeting, housing, and saving, ensuring they feel confident and well-prepared for what lies ahead.

Key Takeaways

- Teach autistic teens the significance of monitoring revenues and expenditures to manage their money better.

- Guide your teen through creating a budget, distinguishing between fixed and variable income, and prioritizing essential expenses.

- Introduce personal finance apps to simplify money management, especially for teens who benefit from visual aids.

- Set up a special needs trust for long-term financial security. You can choose either a first-party or third-party trust, depending on your situation.

- Review and update financial plans regularly to adapt to your teen's changing needs and government benefits landscape.

- Help your teen prepare for independent living by explaining everyday expenses and creating a practical spending plan together.

- Highlight the need to create an emergency fund to address unexpected expenditures and secure financial resilience.

Now that your teen has a solid foundation in financial management, it is time to focus on skills that will help them navigate adulthood beyond just numbers. Promoting self-advocacy and resilience empowers them to make decisions confidently, overcome challenges, and communicate their needs effectively in a world that can feel overwhelming.

Chapter 10:

Promoting Self-Advocacy and Resilience

Imagine your teen, Alex, standing nervously before his science teacher, clutching his project report. He takes a deep breath and says, "I need an extension because the group work was overwhelming." His teacher pauses, then nods in agreement. You would think he just won a championship! That is self-advocacy—asking for what he needs, even when it is tough. Alex might not always get the answer he wants, but building resilience starts with finding his voice.

The next topic is teaching self-advocacy skills—setting the stage for moments like this is where real growth happens.

Teaching Self-Advocacy Skills

Self-advocacy is a vital skill for autistic teenagers as they prepare for adulthood. It means recognizing their right to express their needs, make personal decisions, and take charge of their lives. Developing this skill is essential for building independence and boosting self-confidence. Teens must understand they have a right to speak up about their needs and see the value in their unique perspectives.

You play a crucial role as a parent or caregiver by modeling self-advocacy for your teen. They learn by observing how you handle daily challenges. When you communicate your needs—whether resolving a work issue or making healthcare decisions—you provide real-world examples of effective self-advocacy.

Another step in building this skill is helping your teen learn about their strengths, challenges, and personal preferences. They can better explain their needs when they understand themselves better. This knowledge is powerful—recognizing what makes them unique gives them the confidence to advocate for themselves and make informed choices.

Effective Communication Strategies

Practical communication is necessary for self-advocacy, but autistic teenagers may struggle to express themselves. Teaching them verbal and nonverbal strategies can increase their confidence and help them express their needs more clearly.

Role-playing offers a helpful way to practice. For instance, you can rehearse with your teen how to request extra time from a teacher on an assignment. This exercise allows them to use precise language, maintain eye contact, and practice active listening in a relaxed setting. Repeating these scenarios boosts confidence, making real-life situations feel less overwhelming.

If your teen struggles with verbal communication, try using visual aids or pre-written scripts. Picture cards can help them express emotions or needs, while scripts provide a template for different situations, reducing anxiety. This makes them feel more prepared and empowered.

Body language and facial expressions are essential for effective communication. Motivate your teenager to rehearse in front of a mirror to increase their awareness of their expressions and posture. Teaching verbal and nonverbal communication strategies helps your teen build confidence in social situations and advocate for their needs.

Identifying Personal Needs

Identifying and expressing personal needs is a crucial aspect of self-advocacy in settings like school, work, and social situations. Guide your teen in listing their specific needs for each scenario, whether accommodations at school, adjusted tasks at work, or sensory supports for social activities.

Creating lists makes the process easier. For school, the list could include accommodations such as extended test time or access to a more peaceful workspace. At work, it could outline needs such as flexible scheduling or tasks that align with their strengths. For social settings, it may include strategies to manage sensory overload. These lists empower your teen to communicate their needs confidently.

Encouraging self-reflection is another way to help your teen understand what they need. Consider introducing journaling to explore their ideas and sentiments. Writing about their experiences can help them identify what works for them and what does not. Regular reflection builds a more vital self-awareness, which is crucial for self-advocacy.

You can also guide this process by asking open-ended questions like, "What kind of environment makes you feel comfortable?" or "What situations make you feel anxious?" These conversations deepen your understanding of your teen's needs and help them articulate them more effectively.

Setting Boundaries

Setting healthy boundaries is another essential aspect of self-advocacy. Boundaries help protect emotional and physical well-being. Teaching your teen to set boundaries involves more than just explaining; it requires practice and ongoing support.

Role-playing helps build this skill effectively. For instance, if a friend asks too many personal questions, your teen can respond confidently by saying, "I am not comfortable sharing that," with a respectful but firm tone. Practicing safely boosts their confidence and prepares them for real-life situations.

Communicating your own experiences with setting boundaries is helpful. Describe a situation where you successfully established or handled a boundary when someone crossed your limits. This will demonstrate to your teen that establishing boundaries is a healthy and normal aspect of life.

Creating a home environment where teenagers feel secure in communicating their boundaries is necessary. Listen actively and respond without judgment when they voice a concern. By respecting their limits, you show them that setting boundaries is acceptable and crucial for building healthy relationships.

Promoting self-respect is essential in this process. When your teen values themselves, they can recognize when others cross their boundaries and respond confidently. Acknowledge their efforts and celebrate even the most minor achievements. Doing so strengthens their sense of self-worth and helps them believe they deserve to be respected.

By integrating these skills into daily routines—whether discussing personal space or negotiating responsibilities—you make setting boundaries a natural part of life. As a parent, demonstrating assertive but empathetic boundary-setting shows your teen how to advocate for themselves while respecting others.

We are proceeding on to developing self-esteem and morale. When your teen feels good about themselves, advocating for their needs becomes effortless.

Building Self-Esteem and Confidence

Start building your teen's self-worth by acknowledging and honoring every accomplishment, no matter how small. This is especially important for autistic teens, as they often encounter extraordinary challenges that can affect their confidence. Each acknowledgment strengthens their efforts and helps establish a strong foundation for resilience. One effective method is creating a "Success Wall" at home, where your teen can proudly showcase artwork, projects, or small victories, like organizing their room or navigating social situations. These visual reminders boost their morale and motivate them to keep pushing forward.

Celebrating these achievements publicly, like presenting certificates or awards to family or friends, can add an extra layer of recognition. It does not have to be a huge event—it is about validating the hard work and determination your teen put into reaching their goal. For example, whether your teen improved academically, demonstrated kindness, or managed a difficult social situation, each accomplishment deserves a moment in the spotlight. Celebrations like these show your teen—and others—that persistence and effort are always worth recognizing.

Encourage your teen to reflect on their successes by discussing what went well and how they overcame obstacles. This reinforces that the process, not just the outcome, matters. For instance, if your teen completed a project despite feeling overwhelmed, focus on their perseverance. Over time, they will start to see their strengths and build a habit of recognizing their achievements, which is a crucial step toward boosting self-worth and emotional resilience.

Recognize the small victories, too. Did your teen start a conversation at school for the first time? Or adjust well to a sudden change in their schedule? Celebrate those achievements. Encourage them to keep a "Progress Journal" to write down these successes. This way, they can track their growth and see their progress when future challenges arise.

Positive self-talk is another critical element in building resilience. Teens, especially those with autism, often struggle with negative thoughts, especially in unfamiliar or difficult situations. Counteracting this with positive affirmations like, "I am capable," or "I can handle this" can shift their focus from what they "cannot" do to what they "can". Engage in open conversations about their feelings, especially when things are unplanned. For example, if your teen says, "I am no good at this," help them reframe it as, "This is hard, but I am learning." These subtle changes build a mindset of determination instead of defeat.

As a parent or caregiver, you play a vital role in modeling positive self-talk. Share your experiences when you face setbacks using phrases like, "I am proud of myself for trying" or, "I learned something new today." This shows your teen that making mistakes is okay and highlights that effort is more valuable than perfection. When praising your teen, emphasize their dedication with statements like, "I saw how much effort you put into that project." Focusing on their hard work reinforces a growth mindset, helping them view setbacks as chances to learn and grow.

Social skills development is another critical area to focus on. Social interactions often feel challenging for many autistic teens. Structured activities, such as clubs, hobby groups, or family game nights, offer a safe environment to practice these skills. Role-playing scenarios like starting a conversation or resolving conflicts help build confidence. Breaking down these interactions into smaller steps makes it easier for your teen to handle real-world situations. Motivate them to ask questions if they are uncertain during conversations. With practice, they will become more confident and independent in social settings.

Celebrating these social victories—whether successfully joining a conversation or responding to a social cue—is just as crucial as recognizing academic achievements. These moments contribute significantly to your teen's self-worth and help build resilience. The more they see these milestones as achievements, the more confident they grow.

Mindfulness and self-care are necessary to support emotional balance and resilience. Encourage your teen to use strategies such as deep breathing or guided imagery to handle stress. Create a "self-care toolbox" with relaxing activities like listening to music, drawing, or walking. Incorporating these routines into their daily lives helps them maintain better control over their emotions.

Following a uniform sleep plan, eating healthy meals, and staying physically active are essential habits that build a solid foundation for dynamic well-being. Help your teen discover self-care routines they enjoy, like cooking, crafting, or simply relaxing. When the whole family prioritizes self-care, it creates a cheerful and validating environment.

The next topic is handling setbacks and challenges—learning to navigate these tough moments is where natural resilience develops.

Handling Setbacks and Challenges

Navigating life's ups and downs is an important skill, especially as autistic teenagers transition into adulthood. You play a crucial role in helping them view setbacks as opportunities rather than failures. Begin by reframing challenges. When your teen encounters difficulties, talk through what happened, identify the obstacles, and brainstorm strategies for handling similar situations in the future. Shift the focus from frustration to problem-solving. For example, if they feel overwhelmed by a math project, suggest breaking it into smaller steps or exploring additional resources together. Remind your teen that even the most successful people face challenges, and setbacks are a natural part of growth.

It is essential to nurture problem-solving skills in your teen. Get them involved in activities that encourage thinking through solutions step-by-step. Begin by defining the problem, brainstorming potential solutions, considering pros and cons, and then implementing a plan. For example, if your teen struggles with homework, help them list their assignments, break them into smaller tasks, and create a schedule. Work together to brainstorm creative solutions and inspire them to study various techniques. Celebrate their efforts to boost confidence and help them feel more capable when tackling challenges.

Managing emotions is another essential component when dealing with setbacks. Teaching teens coping strategies like deep breathing, relaxation exercises, or physical activities can help them manage overwhelming emotions. Encourage healthy outlets such as sports, drawing, or listening to music. Journaling can also help your teen process their feelings privately. By modeling these behaviors and being open about your stress, you show them it is normal to feel frustrated sometimes and that there are ways to manage it.

Seeking support is necessary for developing resilience. Help your teen see that they do not have to face challenges alone. A strong family, friends, and mentors network offers valuable guidance and encouragement. Look into mentorship programs where your teen can connect with experienced individuals who share advice and personal stories. Encourage your teen to build community by joining clubs or participating in group activities. Create a safe space at home where your teen feels comfortable discussing their struggles openly and without judgment. Actively listen, validate their emotions, and offer constructive feedback to build trust and resilience.

Sometimes, it is vital to seek professional help. A therapist or counselor can offer support designed for your teen's needs. They work directly with your teen to create personalized strategies for managing emotions and overcoming challenges more effectively.

These strategies—reframing setbacks, building problem-solving skills, teaching emotional regulation, and seeking support—help your teen develop a strong foundation for facing life's challenges with resilience. Begin by viewing challenges as learning opportunities rather than obstacles. For example, if your teen struggles with a test, guide them to evaluate what went wrong and create a plan for better results next time.

Next, build problem-solving skills through activities like puzzles, strategy games, or real-life scenarios where they can practice breaking down issues and thinking creatively. Encourage hobbies that relax and engage them, making stress more straightforward to manage. Regular family check-ins provide a space to discuss emotions and show your teen that everyone has ups and downs.

Finally, remind your teen that seeking support is a strength, not a weakness. Connecting with mentors, participating in group activities, and discussing family issues reinforce that asking for help is okay.

The next topic is encouraging goal-setting and persistence. Resilience also means helping your teen look forward, plan for the future, and stay motivated, even when challenges arise.

Encouraging Goal-Setting and Persistence

Promoting self-advocacy and resilience among autistic teenagers is critical, and a practical way to build these skills is through goal-setting. Teens thrive when they have a clear sense of purpose, and using a structured method like SMART goals (Specific, Measurable, Achievable, Relevant, and Time-bound) helps turn their ambitions into manageable steps. This framework makes it easier for them to set a clear target, measure progress, and stay focused.

To get started, help your teen turn a broad goal like "I want to do better in school" into something specific and achievable. For example, changing it to "I want to raise my math grade from a C to a B by studying an extra hour each day" gives them a clear objective and a way to track success. Make sure each goal fits the SMART criteria: It should be detailed, measurable, and challenging yet doable. Goals must also align with their interests to maintain motivation, and adding a time frame keeps them focused.

Writing down goals strengthens commitment. Encourage your teen to write their plans on paper, turning ideas into concrete steps. Review the goals together, creating a collaborative atmosphere. This approach helps prevent overwhelm and ensures each goal is realistic and achievable.

Life rarely unfolds as expected, making resilience a necessary skill. When setbacks arise—like an injury preventing a teen from achieving a sports goal—guide them to pivot their focus. Instead of giving up, they can concentrate on physical therapy or explore new ways to stay active. This approach shows that adjusting plans is not failing but discovering a different route.

Highlighting real-world examples of individuals who adapted their goals in response to challenges can be helpful, too. Hearing stories of athletes or students who turned obstacles into new opportunities shows teens that setbacks are just detours, not dead-ends.

Recognizing small wins is vital for maintaining strong motivation. Acknowledge each achievement, whether your teen delivers a short presentation to the family or speaks up in a group setting. These moments boost confidence and reinforce the value of their efforts. Use mini-rewards or a visual progress tracker to keep morale high.

It is just as vital to create a validating environment at home. Hold regular family check-ins so your teen can discuss their progress, challenges, and any necessary goal adjustments. When you share your goals as a family, you model positive behavior and demonstrate that everyone, regardless of age, is working toward something.

Your role involves setting goals and empowering your teen to set their own. Ask open-ended questions like, "What are you excited to learn more about?" This approach encourages them to think independently and set goals that match their interests.

Positive reinforcement is also crucial. Focus on praising effort, not just results. Instead of saying, "Great job on the A," say, "I am proud of the hard work you put into that project." This builds a growth mindset, showing them that effort is just as valuable as the outcome.

Schools can support goal-setting by encouraging students to set personal goals, such as improving their presentation skills or tackling new subjects. Connecting goals to future aspirations makes the effort feel more meaningful. For example, if your teen wants to become an engineer, emphasize how today's focus on math and science helps lay the groundwork for their dream.

Reflecting on completed goals is equally important. After achieving a goal, ask your teen what strategies worked and what they would change. This reflection turns experiences into learning opportunities, helping them tackle future goals confidently.

When you guide your teen through setting and adjusting goals, you are not just aiming for success; you are helping them build lifelong skills in self-advocacy and resilience. By offering support, you empower them to face challenges head-on and grow stronger.

Key Takeaways

- Self-advocacy is essential for autistic teenagers because it empowers them to express their needs and make their own decisions.

- Help your teen understand their strengths, challenges, and preferences to build confidence in advocating for themselves.

- Using visual aids or scripts helps teens who find verbal communication challenging feel more prepared and confident.

- Encourage self-reflection through journaling to help teens gain self-awareness about what works for them.

- Use role-playing and share personal experiences to teach boundary-setting in a safe, supportive environment.

- Creating a supportive home environment fosters self-advocacy and helps teens feel safe discussing their boundaries and needs.

- Recognizing progress through verbal praise or visual reminders reinforces effort and perseverance.

- Structured activities and social opportunities provide a safe space for practicing communication and social skills.

- Regular family check-ins allow teens to share their experiences, get support, and adjust their goals.

- Encouraging goal-setting and persistence builds self-advocacy and resilience, empowering teens to navigate challenges.

The next topic is technology and assistive tools. While building self-advocacy and resilience is crucial, leveraging the right tools can amplify your teen's strengths and independence. Technology can be a powerful ally in your teen's journey, from apps that aid communication to devices that support learning.

Chapter 11:

Technology and Assistive Tools

Imagine you just got your teenager a fancy new smartwatch. The goal? To help manage daily routines and reduce those "Wait, what?!" moments. On day one, you are feeling optimistic. You set a reminder for breakfast. The watch buzzes—your teen glances at it and says, "It is breakfast time… but it is also 'ignore your watch' time." You stifle a laugh, realizing that technology can be helpful, too. Still, humor and flexibility might be just as crucial when introducing new tools.

The next topic is using apps for organization and reminders to make daily routines smoother and more predictable for your teen.

Using Apps for Organization and Reminders

One of the most effective ways to help autistic teenagers build routines and manage responsibilities is to introduce organizational apps. These tools can change how your teen approaches everyday tasks, allowing them to grow more independent and confident in handling their daily lives.

Task Management Apps

Task management apps are handy for autistic teens because they break down overwhelming tasks into smaller, more manageable steps. This makes it easier to approach responsibilities without feeling intimidated. For example, an app like Thruday, designed with neurodivergent users in mind, allows teens to create a list of tasks they can break into bite-sized pieces. By visualizing these smaller steps, your teen can better understand what needs to be done and feel a sense of accomplishment as they track their progress.

Many task management apps also have features like color coding, which can help organize tasks based on their priority or type. This visual cue system helps teens by clarifying which tasks they must handle right away and which can wait. Another essential feature of these apps is the ability to set deadlines, encouraging your teen to complete tasks on time while also helping them develop responsibility and discipline.

Scheduling Tools

Scheduling tools, like calendar apps, improve time management and planning. Apps such as Google Calendar provide interactive and visually engaging schedules, making it easier for teens to stay organized and on top of their daily activities. These apps often include color-coded events and can sync with other devices, ensuring that schedules are easily accessible and can be updated whenever needed.

Visual schedules are especially beneficial for autistic teens because they provide a clear and tangible representation of time. Time can often feel like an abstract concept, but seeing their day in front of them helps your teen mentally and physically prepare for tasks and appointments. Prioritization features within these tools also help emphasize essential tasks, ensuring your teen focuses on what truly matters throughout their day.

Note-Taking Applications

Another handy resource is note-taking apps, which allow for flexible recording and organization of information. Evernote is a popular option that offers a wide range of features, enabling teens to capture notes, organize them efficiently, and sync them across multiple devices. Your teen can easily capture essential details anytime and anywhere, helping prevent them from forgetting crucial information.

The benefits of note-taking apps go beyond just writing notes. With features like document scanning, character recognition, and the ability to integrate with other apps like Google Drive or Microsoft Teams, note-taking apps are a powerful tool for school and personal use. Your teen can create detailed study notes, map their thoughts for upcoming projects, and share notes with teachers or peers for better collaboration.

Reminder Systems

Setting reminders is an excellent way to boost memory and accountability for autistic teens. Apps that allow customizable alarms and notifications can gently remind your teen about daily routines and essential tasks. An app like Stay Focused limits distractions by blocking unnecessary apps and includes reminder options, giving your teen structure while encouraging productivity.

You can tailor these customizable alarms to fit your teen's specific needs, whether to remind them to do homework, take medication, or follow their morning routine. These gentle nudges help keep them on track without feeling overwhelmed. Recurring reminders also create a sense of consistency, which can be a powerful tool for building and sticking to healthy routines over time.

The next topic covers assistive communication devices, which can significantly improve your teen's interaction with others and expression of needs.

Assistive Communication Devices

Assistive communication technologies can be life-changing for nonverbal or minimally verbal autistic teenagers. These tools allow teens to express their needs, thoughts, and emotions, helping them communicate more effectively and confidently in social and academic settings.

Speech Generating Devices (SGDs) are powerful tools that significantly enhance communication. These electronic devices convert selected words or symbols into spoken language, making them ideal for nonverbal teens. For instance, your teen can use an SGD to request a bathroom break at school, avoiding confusion or frustration. What makes these devices even more valuable is their customization options. You can adjust the vocabulary, symbols, and layout to fit your teen's preferences, making it feel personal and relevant. This adaptability helps them communicate naturally and comfortably.

Another flexible option is tablet-based apps for Augmentative and Alternative Communication (AAC). Apps like PECSTalk™ incorporate traditional communication systems but add the convenience of modern technology. These apps use visual aids, symbols, and easy-to-use interfaces to accommodate different skill levels. What is great is that they can be updated frequently, reflecting your teen's changing needs. Since they run on standard tablets, they blend in more seamlessly daily, reducing the risk of stigma. Teens may find these apps less intimidating to use, and the ability to adapt the interface helps maintain their engagement and motivation.

Text-to-speech software is powerful for teens who can type but struggle to speak. It converts written words into spoken sentences, allowing your teen to share their thoughts in group settings, like a classroom discussion. Imagine your teen typing their input during a lesson, and the software speaks it aloud—ensuring their voice is heard and respected. This technology boosts participation and confidence by bridging the gap between written and spoken language, making it easier for teens to contribute meaningfully in social and educational environments.

The Picture Exchange Communication System (PECS) uses images to help teenagers build independent communication skills. PECS starts with primary exchanges, like handing over a picture to request a snack, and gradually advances to form sentences. This structured approach helps teens who struggle with abstract verbal concepts by giving them a concrete way to express themselves. Because it progressively builds skills, teens gain confidence at every stage, reducing frustration and encouraging more complex communication.

Keep a few strategies in mind to maximize the effectiveness of these tools. For Speech-Generating Devices, involve your teen in choosing vocabulary and symbols to make the device feel like their own. Regularly updating the content to include new interests or relevant phrases keeps communication engaging and authentic. Training family members and teachers also ensure everyone is on the same page, promoting consistent use across settings.

Evaluate your teen's learning style and communication needs when using AAC apps. Choosing an app with adaptable features allows it to grow with your teen's vocabulary and preferences. During structured lessons or informal daily chats, practice is critical to naturally integrating the app into your teen's routine. Regular technical support and updates will keep the app functioning smoothly so your teen can rely on it for communication.

For text-to-speech software, encourage your teen to use it for multiple activities like class assignments, social messages, and even creative writing. This variety builds comfort and fluency, making transitioning between academic and social scenarios easier. Using this tool regularly will help your teen find their voice in a broader range of settings.

When introducing PECS, start with images of items your teen loves, like favorite foods or toys, to spark immediate interest. Watch how they respond to various pictures and slowly add new ones as they show more comfort. Collaboration with a trained PECS professional can provide extra support and guidance, ensuring a smooth learning experience.

The next topic is educational software and resources, which can provide your teen with engaging, personalized tools to support their learning and development.

Educational Software and Resources

Choosing the right educational software for autistic teenagers goes beyond finding the latest tech; it is about creating opportunities for independence, learning, and personal growth. With the right tools, your teen can develop crucial skills that are engaging and tailored to their needs.

Interactive Learning Platforms

Interactive learning platforms have completely changed how autistic teens engage with academic content. By turning lessons into interactive games, these platforms make learning both fun and motivating. Many include rewards, badges, and levels, providing instant feedback and encouraging progress. Teens can work through lessons independently, shaping a learning experience that meets their needs.

For instance, platforms like Vizzle offer visual lessons paired with interactive activities, making them ideal for reinforcing key concepts. The platform's ability to track progress and differentiate learning helps ensure your teen gets the right level of support. Because these platforms feel more like games than traditional lessons, they also reduce the stress of more structured classroom environments.

When choosing interactive learning tools, focus on features like adjustable difficulty levels, customizable settings, and real-time feedback. These options help tailor the experience, keeping your teen engaged and on track.

Visual Learning Tools

Visual learning tools are essential for many autistic teens, as they cater to their strengths in visual processing. These tools use images, colors, and text to simplify complex concepts, making them easier for teens to understand and remember. Visual aids can include anything from infographics and diagrams to video tutorials, breaking down information in a transparent and manageable way.

Pictello is a great example of an app that lets you create personalized social stories with pictures and text. These stories help teens understand various social situations and navigate complex concepts.

Similarly, First Then Visual Schedule HD uses visual schedules to support daily task completion and self-direction.

To get the most out of visual tools, break big topics into smaller chunks, use color coding for clarity, and maintain consistent visual cues across lessons. This approach strengthens understanding and helps your teen feel more organized and confident.

Study Aid Applications

Study aid apps can make a massive difference in reinforcing learning and building strong study habits. Tools like digital flashcards, quizzes, and repetition-based activities are ideal for helping teens master new concepts through consistent review.

For example, Quizlet allows you to create custom flashcards and quizzes, letting your teen practice at their own pace. This repetitive structure is especially effective for autistic teens who might struggle with working memory. To maximize the benefits, set aside regular study times and encourage your teen to review materials in small, consistent intervals. This prevents overwhelm and promotes better knowledge retention.

Online Tutoring Services

Online tutoring provides a personalized learning experience that can significantly impact autistic teenagers. By contacting specialized tutors, your teen can receive one-on-one support tailored to their needs and interests. These tutors adjust the pace, introduce engaging topics, and build sessions around your teen's strengths.

For instance, TeachTown Social Skills provides structured lessons through animated video content, focusing on social and academic skills. With flexible scheduling, online tutoring can fit easily into your routine, making learning accessible and enjoyable.

Choose online tutors who have experience working with teenagers on the autism spectrum. Look for platforms that include interactive features, such as screen sharing and digital whiteboards, to keep sessions engaging.

Guidelines for Using Educational Software

When using educational software for your teen, having clear guidelines can make a big difference in their learning experience. Below are some strategies to maximize the benefits of these tools, ensuring they stay engaged and motivated while using them.

- **Consistency:** Incorporate these tools into your teen's daily routine. Regular use builds familiarity and enhances engagement.

- **Customization:** Adjust settings to fit your teen's learning style. Include topics that interest them and tweak difficulty levels as needed.

- **Interactive Features:** Choose software with elements like quizzes, real-time feedback, or gamification to maintain interest and motivation.

- **Parental Involvement:** Your involvement can boost success. Celebrate progress, offer support, and discuss what your teen enjoys or struggles with.

- **Monitor Progress:** Use tracking features to pinpoint strengths and areas needing improvement. This insight will help tailor future learning activities.

- **Balanced Approach:** Blend digital tools with hands-on learning and social interactions to create a well-rounded educational experience.

The next topic covers the benefits of telehealth services, another powerful tool for supporting your teen's social, emotional, and educational development.

Benefits of Telehealth Services

Telehealth has redefined how autistic teenagers access health care, making it more manageable for families. Traditional in-person visits can present unique challenges, so virtual platforms offer a stress-free alternative that suits many teens' needs. Connecting online from the comfort of home reduces the sensory overload that often accompanies trips to medical facilities, such as unfamiliar sights, sounds, and routines.

Telehealth stands out for its accessibility. Teens struggling with travel can skip the stress entirely through virtual appointments. You no longer have to navigate busy streets or sit in crowded waiting rooms. Instead, your teen can engage comfortably from their room, leading to a more positive interaction with their healthcare provider. This environment encourages open communication, which leads to improved care.

Telehealth also supports continuity of care, which is critical for autistic teenagers. Regular, predictable check-ins allow healthcare providers to monitor health concerns closely and adjust treatment plans quickly based on real-time updates. You are not dealing with scattered, rushed appointments but getting consistent, thoughtful care that aligns with your teen's needs. This consistent engagement makes it easier to track progress and keep healthcare routines on track without the usual disruptions of scheduling and logistics.

Another significant advantage is broader access to specialists. Many families struggle to find local healthcare providers with a deep understanding of autism spectrum disorder (ASD). With telehealth, geographical barriers no longer stand in the way. You can connect with specialized professionals from anywhere in another city or country. Your teen can receive high-quality, personalized care without settling for a generalist. You can connect directly with experts with the experience and knowledge to offer the most effective support.

Routine building is another area where telehealth can be a game-changer. Autistic teens often rely on structure, and regular virtual sessions create a consistent pattern that fits easily into their schedules. Knowing when to expect appointments helps build accountability and makes health care part of their routine rather than an occasional disruption. This consistency fosters a sense of security and helps reinforce healthy habits over time.

Comfort is a huge factor, too. When your teen is in a familiar environment, they will likely feel less guarded and more relaxed. This comfort translates into more honest conversations about their health, essential for effective treatment. Healthcare providers gain a clearer picture of what is happening, leading to better diagnoses and tailored treatment plans. Being at home, surrounded by their favorite items, gives your teen the confidence to express themselves more openly.

Reducing stress is another compelling reason to choose telehealth. Traditional visits can be anxiety-inducing for autistic teenagers because of the long waits, unfamiliar routines, and sensory overload. By shifting appointments to the home environment, telehealth removes these stress triggers. This leads to a calmer, more constructive session where your teen can engage more fully without the anxiety of being in an uncomfortable setting.

And it is not just the teens who benefit. Telehealth has significant perks for parents and caregivers, too. You are not scrambling to fit appointments into a busy day, manage other children, or take time off work. Virtual visits are more straightforward to accommodate, letting you be more present during sessions without upending your schedule. Plus, many telehealth programs offer parent training, helping you learn strategies to better support your teen's development right from home. This convenience makes a big difference, allowing you to be actively involved in a way that does not add stress.

Telehealth's flexibility also sets it apart. You can adapt sessions to your teen's needs and preferences through video calls, messaging apps, or other digital tools. You are not dealing with the distractions of a busy clinic, so sessions are more focused and productive. Providers can tailor their approach to what works best for your teen, ensuring each interaction feels meaningful and effective.

Research shows that teens and families tend to stick with telehealth programs longer than in-person options (MacMillan, 2021). The ease and accessibility of virtual care reduce dropouts, leading to better outcomes. Your teen gets a sustained support system that consistently addresses their needs, helping them build a healthier, more stable routine.

While telehealth may not replace all face-to-face interactions—certain aspects of care might still require in-person visits—the overwhelming benefits make it a powerful addition to your teen's healthcare plan. Advancements in technology will keep enhancing telehealth, introducing new tools and features to support autistic teenagers better. With these innovations, families can count on accessible, compassionate care wherever they are.

Key Takeaways

- Smartwatches can help autistic teens manage routines but require humor and flexibility when introducing new tools.

- Task management apps break down complex tasks into smaller steps, making them less overwhelming and more achievable.

- Note-taking apps help teens quickly capture, organize, and recall information, supporting academic and personal use.

- Assistive communication devices enable nonverbal or minimally verbal teens to express their needs effectively.

- Text-to-speech software converts typed words into speech, allowing participation in discussions.

- Educational software like interactive learning platforms and visual tools cater to unique learning styles.

- Visual learning tools leverage strengths in visual processing to simplify complex concepts.

- Online tutoring services offer personalized support, connecting teens with specialized tutors.

- Telehealth provides accessible, stress-free health care from home, reducing the sensory challenges of in-person visits.

Now that you have equipped your teen with practical tools and strategies, the next chapter focuses on creating a safe and supportive home environment. Building this foundation is essential for fostering your teen's well-being and growth, ensuring they feel secure, understood, and empowered daily.

Chapter 12:

Creating a Safe and Supportive Home Environment

You walk into the living room, exhausted after a long day, only to find your autistic teenager sitting on the couch with an entire tower of couch cushions stacked neatly beside them. "What is going on?" you ask, raising an eyebrow. "Just needed a quiet spot," they reply casually, peeking out from their cushion fort. You cannot help but laugh. Who knew couch cushions could be so versatile? As they burrow deeper, you realize it is more than just quirky behavior—their way of creating a sense of safety and calm. Creating that safe space is essential, but adapting your home for sensory needs takes it a step further.

Adapting the Home Space for Sensory Needs

Creating a sensory-friendly home environment is beneficial not only for autistic teenagers but also for you, the parent or caregiver. You feel relieved knowing your teen is safe and comfortable at home. This environment helps reduce their stress, promotes their focus, and fosters their independence. Adapting the space to suit their sensory needs creates a comfortable atmosphere that reduces overwhelming stimuli. Research shows that autistic teenagers often experience heightened sensory sensitivity, which can impact their daily participation and emotional well-being (Wang, 2024). Providing a supportive environment reassures you and brings peace of mind.

Creating sensory-friendly zones throughout the home is a highly effective strategy. These designated areas serve as safe retreats where teens can escape to decompress and self-regulate when feeling overwhelmed. You can create a tactile-friendly space that minimizes discomfort by choosing calming colors like soft blues or greens and incorporating soft textures like cotton or fleece. This reduces stress, promotes focus, and fosters independence, enhancing the teenager's emotional well-being.

In these sensory zones, consider managing sound sensitivity by using noise-canceling headphones or installing soundproof curtains to block out disruptive noises. Autistic teens often have heightened auditory perception, making daily sounds like a refrigerator hum or a neighbor's barking dog seem unbearably loud. Creating a quiet area with white noise machines can help mask unpleasant noises, promoting a sense of calm and focus.

Adding sensory-friendly products can also make a big difference. Weighted blankets, for instance, provide deep pressure stimulation, which researchers have shown to reduce stress and improve sleep quality for many teens with sensory sensitivities (Danoff-Burg et al., 2020). Fidget tools offer a physical outlet for excess energy, helping teens maintain concentration during tasks.

Managing environmental stimuli is another crucial aspect. Lighting, for example, can be a source of distress if it is too bright or flickers. Replace harsh fluorescent lights with softer, dimmable options to create a more visually comfortable space. Reducing unwanted odors using unscented cleaning products or installing air purifiers can also make the home more sensory-friendly.

Personalizing the space is equally important. Allowing teens to select colors, furniture, or wall art helps them connect with their environment and feel more in control. For instance, a teen who loves space might find a room decorated with celestial-themed decor comforting and engaging. This personalization fosters a sense of ownership, helping to promote independence and emotional well-being.

Implementing these strategies requires more than just observation and decision-making. It requires open communication and collaboration.

Ask your teen which sensory inputs they find calming or overwhelming, and include them in the decision-making process whenever possible. This collaborative approach validates their preferences and encourages self-advocacy, a critical skill for navigating the world as they grow older. It also fosters a sense of connection and involvement, making you feel more engaged in your teen's life and well-being.

Helping your teen navigate daily routines is the next step in creating a balanced, supportive environment. Establishing consistent routines offers stability and allows teens to manage transitions and unexpected changes quickly. These routines are tasks and tools that empower your teen to feel more confident and secure. Predictability helps them feel more in control and lowers their anxiety because they know what to expect.

Establishing Routines and Structure

Consistent routines create a safe and supportive environment for autistic teenagers by offering structure and reducing anxiety. Visual schedules effectively establish these routines, helping teens feel more secure. They outline daily activities clearly, assisting teens to understand what to expect and making transitions easier. Visual schedules can use pictures, icons, or even written descriptions to illustrate each part of the day. For instance, a morning schedule might start with an image of breakfast, followed by pictures for school time, lunch, and any other activities.

Visual schedules play a significant role in increasing independence for autistic teenagers. By reducing their reliance on verbal prompts from adults, these schedules allow them to look at the schedule and anticipate what is next. A study by Banda, Grimmett, and Hart found that visual schedules improved engagement and minimized behavioral challenges, particularly during transitions, in classroom settings (Banda & Grimmett, 2008).

Consistency is another critical factor in creating effective routines. Keeping the same sequence of activities each day can provide stability, help your teen feel in control, and reduce the chances of emotional outbursts. Predictable routines build security and boost self-confidence by helping teens understand expectations and anticipate what will happen next. This can reduce power struggles and allow for smoother transitions throughout the day.

However, maintaining strict routines does not mean no room for flexibility. Allowing small changes in the structure can help autistic teens adapt to unexpected events without feeling overwhelmed. For example, if lunch is usually at noon but has to be moved to 11:30 one day, using a visual schedule to indicate the shift can help the teen adjust more comfortably. Research suggests that this gradual introduction to change while maintaining the core structure benefits autistic teens (Kesherim, 2024).

Another vital aspect of creating effective routines is incorporating scheduled breaks. Regular downtime can prevent sensory overload and reduce stress, which is especially important for teens with sensory sensitivities. For instance, if your teenager struggles with transitions, adding a short break for a calming activity, such as listening to music or engaging with a sensory toy, can help them recharge before tackling the next task.

It is also beneficial to involve your teenager in creating these schedules. When teens feel a sense of control and ownership over their day, they are more likely to stick to the routine. Some teenagers prefer simple, icon-based schedules, while others respond better to detailed written plans. By tailoring the visual schedules to their preferences and comprehension levels, you are ensuring they can use them effectively, even during times of stress.

You can apply visual schedules to daily activities and manage unexpected changes. For example, if the weather prevents outdoor playtime, having a visual alternative like "indoor play" on the schedule can provide a sense of continuity and reduce anxiety. A structured environment, including planned changes, can help autistic teenagers feel more in control and better equipped to handle life's uncertainties.

Creating predictable routines, however, is just one part of fostering a safe environment. It would be best if you addressed specific risks at home to ensure safety, and developing an emergency plan tailored to your teen's unique needs is an essential step in this process. It ensures everyone knows what to do if unexpected situations arise, providing additional peace of mind.

Safety Measures and Emergency Planning

Implementing robust safety protocols for autistic teenagers involves creating a detailed plan, teaching essential safety skills, and tailoring strategies to meet unique needs. Start by identifying potential emergencies—fire, medical crises, or wandering—and establish a clear plan that lists emergency contacts and safe spaces. According to Autism Speaks, elopement (wandering) and miscommunication can pose significant risks, making proactive planning essential (*Wandering Prevention*, n.d.).

Developing safety skills through role-play is effective. Regular practice helps teens internalize routines like answering the door safely or recognizing hazardous situations. Integrating real-life simulations, like visiting local emergency services, can help familiarize teens with unfamiliar environments and personnel, reducing anxiety during emergencies.

Customize communication strategies. If your teen uses augmentative and alternative communication (AAC) devices, ensure they are comfortable using them in emergencies. Reinforce emergency phrases like "I need help" or "I am lost" so they can express themselves clearly under stress. Visual aids like maps or written schedules can also help teens anticipate and respond to changing circumstances, reducing the risk of panic.

Environmental safety is equally crucial. Teach your teen about potential hazards inside and outside the home. Visual cues (like hazard symbols) can help reinforce which areas are off-limits. People often overlook environmental risks when planning for safety. Still, small changes—like child-proofing electrical outlets or adding soft padding to sharp furniture edges—can make a big difference. Frequent neighborhood walks or practice outings to public spaces can build confidence and awareness of the surroundings.

Managing sensory needs adds another layer of safety because autistic teens often experience heightened sensitivities that can cause distress during emergencies. Incorporating familiar sensory tools, like noise-canceling headphones or weighted blankets, can help keep them calm. Introducing new stimuli gradually and practicing with emergency sounds (like smoke alarms) can prepare your teen for unexpected situations.

Finally, regular reviews and updates to the safety plan are essential as your teen grows and their needs change. Autism Speaks recommends updating safety plans annually or after significant life changes to ensure protocols stay relevant and practical.

Once you have a solid safety foundation, involving autistic teens in household chores can help build their independence and life skills.

Encouraging Participation in Household Chores

Involving autistic teenagers in household chores is a valuable way to foster independence and teach essential life skills. Household responsibilities help teens develop self-confidence and prepare them for more independent adult living. According to Autism Speaks, starting early with simple tasks and gradually increasing complexity can build comfort and proficiency (*Life Skills*, n.d.).

Choose chores that align with your teen's strengths and preferences to make the process effective. Some teenagers may prefer repetitive tasks like folding laundry or organizing items, which can help them develop focus and routine. Others might enjoy creative tasks like cooking or gardening. The goal is to observe their natural inclinations and choose chores that feel rewarding instead of overwhelming. Introducing life skills in this way can promote their autonomy and enhance self-esteem.

Using visual aids can also significantly improve understanding and consistency. Many autistic teens respond well to visual supports such as chore charts, checklists, and color-coded schedules. Visual cues provide clarity and reduce anxiety around unpredictability, making it easier for them to complete tasks with minimal verbal guidance. For example, a visual countdown or a "first/then" board helps set expectations and transitions, making it easier for them to know what to expect next.

Break down tasks into small, manageable steps when teaching new skills through household chores. For example, instead of saying, "Clean the kitchen," break it into individual steps like "Wash the dishes," "Wipe the counter," and "Sweep the floor." This step-by-step approach provides clear direction, making the process more structured and less overwhelming. When teens have structured and consistent routines, they feel more in control and experience less anxiety.

Involving teens in decision-making around chores can also be empowering. Allowing them to choose which tasks they prefer or how they want to organize their schedule respects their preferences and promotes self-determination. This collaborative approach can increase their willingness to participate and build decision-making skills.

Positive reinforcement is another critical strategy. Celebrating small achievements with praise, stickers, or privileges, like choosing the family's evening movie, can go a long way. For teens who understand language well, you can also explain the impact of their actions—for example, how keeping a space tidy makes it easier to find things later. Such recognition reinforces their sense of contribution and creates a positive association with household responsibilities.

Modifying chores to suit their needs can also make a big difference. If sorting laundry by colors feels overwhelming, simplify it by just sorting light and dark clothes. Or, if vacuuming is too much due to sensory sensitivities, offer alternatives like using a handheld duster. Tailoring tasks ensures the responsibilities remain within their comfort zone while promoting growth.

Creating consistency is vital. Establishing a regular time each day or week for chores can build a sense of routine and predictability, which many autistic teens find comforting. Over time, these routines can become second nature, making it easier for them to adapt to similar structures in other areas of life.

Remember that teaching life skills through household chores is not just about completing tasks but nurturing independence and building a foundation for future success. Every small step, whether setting the table or feeding the family pet, contributes to developing skills they will use throughout their lives. Adapting strategies to fit their strengths and preferences, you are helping your teen gain practical skills and boost their confidence and self-worth.

Key Takeaways

- Creating a sensory-friendly home environment reduces stress, promotes focus, and supports independence for autistic teenagers.

- Manage environmental stimuli using dimmable lighting, reducing odors, and minimizing harsh sounds.

- Establishing structured routines with visual schedules increases predictability and independence.

- Consistency and flexibility in routines provide stability while allowing teens to adapt to unexpected changes.

- Creating detailed safety plans and teaching safety skills are essential for addressing specific risks at home.

- Involving teens in household chores fosters independence, life skills, and self-confidence.

- Use visual aids like chore charts and checklists to support task completion and reduce anxiety.

- Allow teens to choose chores to promote self-determination and decision-making skills.

- Consistency in chore routines helps build predictable habits, supporting independence over time.

As you build a supportive environment and routines that empower your autistic teen, each small success becomes a milestone worth celebrating. Celebrating every achievement, big or small, boosts their confidence and supports their growth. Now, let us explore how celebrating these moments helps build momentum for their future success.

Chapter 13:

Celebrating Achievements and Looking Ahead

You remember the moment your teen finally tied their shoelaces on their own. It was not just a basic knot—this was a reason to celebrate! After weeks of crouching down, untangling knots, and offering encouragement, that confident smile appeared as the bow stayed in place. You exchanged proud looks, knowing it was never just about the laces. It represented persistence and confidence. While others might see it as a minor achievement, you know each milestone is a victory worth celebrating.

Recognizing these moments sets the foundation for appreciating each unique milestone along their journey.

Acknowledging Milestones and Achievements

Recognizing accomplishments motivates autistic teens by boosting confidence, reinforcing positive behaviors, and paving the way for future success. Recognizing each small milestone boosts self-esteem and encourages greater independence. Research shows that celebrating small wins triggers the brain's reward system to release dopamine, which boosts mood and motivation, creating a positive cycle that drives teens to set and achieve new goals (Bergland, 2013).

Celebrating Small Wins

The power of celebrating small victories lies in how these moments accumulate into more considerable achievements over time. Something that might seem minor—such as your teen initiating a conversation or completing a daily task—can be monumental for autistic teens. These instances deserve recognition because they represent tangible progress. According to Psychology Today, recognizing small successes activates the brain's "dopamine spritz," a rewarding feeling that boosts confidence and makes it more likely that your teen will continue pursuing new goals (Selig, 2012).

Dividing big goals into smaller, manageable steps helps your teen experience success more frequently. For instance, when learning to navigate public transportation, celebrate each step—like checking the bus schedule or boarding alone—to reinforce their progress. Use praise, stickers, or small rewards to maintain their motivation.

Documenting Progress

Keeping a record of your teen's achievements, whether through journaling, digital tracking apps, or visual tools like charts, is an excellent way to motivate and track progress. Documenting wins gives you and your teen a visual representation of their growth, helping reinforce accomplishments and maintain motivation. Research highlights that reflecting on progress can help autistic teens recognize their development over time, which they may not always perceive on their own (Hutten, 2015).

A "success journal" can motivate your teen by letting them record achievements like finishing homework, learning new skills, or helping with household chores. Reviewing past successes over time allows them to see their resilience and progress. Keep the focus positive, and celebrate every effort, no matter how small.

Involving Peers and Family

Sharing achievements with others makes celebrating them even more impactful. Including family, peers, or teachers in recognizing milestones can strengthen your teen's sense of belonging and pride. When autistic teens feel supported by their community, it enhances their self-esteem and fosters a greater understanding of connection. A small family gathering, a note of praise from a teacher, or a group activity with peers to celebrate a new achievement can make these moments even more special.

Social reinforcement shows that positive feedback from a group creates a ripple effect, validating individual efforts and building a network of support. So, whether it is a sibling congratulating them or a teacher acknowledging their efforts, these external validations reinforce their achievements and encourage them to keep striving for more.

Using Visual Reminders

For autistic teens, who may find abstract concepts like success challenging to grasp, visual aids are a powerful tool for making their accomplishments feel tangible. Seeing progress visually, through achievement boards or charts, helps track growth and is a daily reminder of their capabilities and hard work.

Setting up an achievement board in their room or using stickers and badges to mark each goal they meet, such as attending a social event or completing a task independently, can be incredibly motivating. This visual representation of their progress is a source of pride and encouragement to keep setting and achieving goals. Each addition to the board becomes a small victory they can see and feel proud of.

The Impact of Positive Reinforcement

Recognizing small wins boosts your teen's sense of capability. Consistent positive reinforcement builds a supportive environment, empowering your teen to tackle challenges confidently. Celebrating each step forward goes beyond acknowledging their achievements—strengthening their confidence to take on more significant future challenges.

By consistently celebrating even the most minor efforts, you help your teen develop a positive outlook on their abilities, encouraging them to persist even when faced with setbacks. These acknowledgments lay the foundation for ongoing growth and success, whether through a simple word of praise, a family celebration, or a visual chart of progress.

Positive reinforcement is essential in guiding your teen's progress. Knowing and applying it can change how you encourage behaviors and nurture independence. Here is how positive reinforcement benefits your teen and how it actively strengthens their growth and confidence.

Importance of Positive Reinforcement

Positive reinforcement helps autistic teens stay motivated, boost their confidence, and support their growth. By using thoughtful and consistent reinforcement strategies, you can support their development across various areas of life. Let us break down some techniques to boost their persistence and sense of accomplishment.

Effective Reinforcement Strategies

Consistency and specificity are essential when using positive reinforcement with teens. A simple way to start is with verbal praise. But instead of a general "Good job," try something more specific like, "You did a fantastic job organizing your schoolwork today!" This approach helps them identify the recognized behavior, making the praise more impactful. Such targeted feedback strengthens the connection between effort and result, encouraging them to repeat positive behaviors.

For younger teens, tangible rewards like small tokens, extra screen time, or favorite snacks can be powerful motivators. A token economy system, where teens earn tokens for desired behaviors and exchange them for privileges, can effectively sustain engagement. In classrooms, visual tools like progress charts add structure and help keep teens engaged by making their achievements visible.

It is vital to balance external rewards with verbal praise and encouragement gradually. Research shows that this approach actively helps teens develop intrinsic motivation (Elias, 2016). They start valuing the satisfaction of completing a task for its own sake rather than relying solely on external incentives.

Setting Clear Goals

To make positive reinforcement more compelling, set clear and attainable goals. Autistic teens need to understand what they are aiming to achieve clearly. For example, set a goal like "Submit all homework assignments on time for a week," which gives a specific and measurable target. Reward their success meaningfully by planning a special outing or engaging in a favorite activity together.

Engage your teen by involving them in goal-setting, which increases their motivation and commitment. Giving them a voice in what they want to accomplish helps them take ownership of the process. Break larger goals into smaller tasks to create manageable steps, making achieving frequent successes easier and providing consistent positive reinforcement.

Encouraging Self-Reflection

Fostering self-reflection in teens is another crucial element of positive reinforcement. Self-reflection helps them connect their efforts to outcomes, promoting a growth mindset and emotional resilience. You can encourage reflection through simple activities like journaling or creating visual collages to capture their accomplishments. For example, after your teen reaches a milestone, ask them to reflect on the strategies that helped them succeed and how they felt throughout the process. This allows them to see setbacks as part of learning and boosts their emotional resilience.

Regular check-ins create opportunities for self-reflection. Discuss what went well and what did not to track progress and build problem-solving skills, which gives your teen more control over their learning.

Building a Reward System

A structured reward system helps sustain motivation and creates a positive experience around reaching goals. Offer short-term rewards for immediate reinforcement, such as selecting a family movie or earning extra playtime. Use more significant rewards like a memorable day trip or new hobby supplies for long-term achievements. Always give rewards immediately after achieving the goal to strengthen the link between effort and results.

Balancing external rewards with verbal praise over time helps promote intrinsic motivation. Teens value their progress more when you gradually replace tangible rewards with verbal recognition instead of just striving for a prize.

Creating a Supportive Environment

Creating an environment that prioritizes effort and persistence over perfection is essential. Celebrating small wins strengthens confidence and encourages positive behavior. Research shows that autistic teens respond well to consistent reinforcement because it lowers anxiety and creates a positive learning space (Sawisz, 2023). Maintaining consistency also builds trust, crucial to reliable support as teens face new challenges.

Positive reinforcement can significantly impact your teen's growth when used thoughtfully and consistently. It is not just about rewarding good behavior; it is about helping them build resilience, learn from mistakes, and develop a more profound sense of self-worth. Integrating these strategies into their daily routines will support their journey toward greater independence and confidence.

Establishing a solid foundation now prepares your teen for lifelong learning and development. Prioritize continuous learning and growth to ensure these reinforcement strategies effectively support their long-term skill development.

Planning for Continuous Learning

Lifelong learning and skill-building are vital in helping autistic teens transition into adulthood, supporting their path to independence, and improving their quality of life. However, many autistic teens have limited access to education, employment, and community activities. Research reveals that nearly 40% of teens and young adults with autism spend little to no time with friends, highlighting the importance of personalized learning experiences that foster skill growth and social engagement (*Autism Spectrum*, 2024).

Identifying Areas for Growth

The first step in promoting lifelong learning is helping teens identify their strengths and areas for improvement. Self-assessment tools like interest inventories and skill-based questionnaires can be practical. This process boosts self-awareness and encourages a sense of ownership in their learning. Providing structured feedback during self-assessment can motivate autistic teens to participate actively in their growth.

For example, if your teen has a knack for art, exploring graphic design or digital art programs can help expand their skills while identifying potential career paths. Regular discussions about their findings can build confidence and strengthen their decision-making abilities.

Exploring Learning Opportunities

Once you identify strengths and interests, it is time to connect your teen with suitable learning resources. Community programs, online courses, and hands-on workshops offer various avenues to develop new skills. Community-based programs, like those provided by local autism organizations, often cater to different interests and abilities, offering cooking, gardening, or photography classes that teach valuable life skills while promoting social interaction.

Coursera, Khan Academy, and Udemy provide flexible learning options that suit various learning styles and needs. Teens can complete these courses to earn certificates, adding credibility to their skills. The adaptable format makes these platforms an excellent fit for students overwhelmed in traditional classrooms.

Beyond digital resources, mentorship or apprenticeship programs provide real-world experience. Working with a mentor in a field of interest can build practical skills and offer opportunities to practice communication and teamwork. Autistic teens who engage in community-based learning experience improved self-esteem and increased engagement in social activities.

Creating a Personalized Learning Plan

Establishing a structured learning plan with clear, measurable goals helps maximize these opportunities. Work with your teen to set short-term targets, like completing an introductory course, and build toward more advanced objectives, such as mastering a skill or exploring career options. For example, if your teen shows interest in technology, begin with an introductory coding class and set a long-term goal to develop a simple app.

Involve your teen in goal-setting to promote self-advocacy and independence. Regularly review and update the plan to align with their evolving interests and abilities. This approach builds their flexibility and resilience, encouraging them to view learning as a continuous process.

Encouraging a Lifelong Learning Mindset

The goal is to nurture a mindset that sees learning as a continuous journey, not just a task for academic or career achievements. Parents and caregivers can make a substantial impact by modeling this behavior. Share what you are learning, whether a new hobby or an interesting topic, to demonstrate that growth happens at every stage of life.

Incorporate learning into daily routines to build skills naturally. For instance, use a grocery shopping trip to teach budgeting and nutrition by having your teen research recipes, plan a shopping list, and handle the budget. This method blends practical life skills with problem-solving and critical thinking.

Engaging in hobbies like sports, arts, and music supports personal growth. Learning an instrument enhances cognitive and motor skills, while team sports build collaboration and perseverance. Participating in structured extracurricular activities boosts teens' confidence. It helps them feel more connected to their community.

Lifelong learning creates new opportunities and boosts confidence in overcoming future challenges. Staying open-minded and flexible will help your teen thrive as they navigate adolescence and adulthood. Embracing different paths and being receptive to unexpected opportunities can pave the way for a brighter future.

Keeping an Open Mind About the Future

Helping autistic teens build flexibility and resilience can be challenging. Still, it is crucial to prepare them to navigate life's uncertainties confidently. Parents and caregivers play a vital role in fostering these skills, guiding teens to adapt more comfortably when facing new situations.

Fostering a Flexible Attitude

Flexibility and adaptability are life skills that can help your teen navigate unexpected changes with less anxiety. Autistic teens often struggle when routines change, making adaptability an essential focus for their development. Gradual introduction to minor adjustments in daily routines can help. For example, you might consider altering the order of morning activities or planning a surprise family outing. Discussing these changes beforehand and explaining their benefits can reduce stress, making it easier for your teen to embrace flexibility as part of everyday life.

Encouraging your teen to reflect on these experiences can further strengthen their adaptability. Creating a "to be" list, focusing on values like patience or persistence, can be a foundation. Promoting self-reflection enhances adaptability as teens become more aware of how they handle different situations and recognize the growth that results from new experiences.

Encouraging Exploration and Curiosity

Encourage autistic teens to explore new activities like playing an instrument, joining a sport, or studying a new subject to spark curiosity and promote growth. Offer support by treating mistakes as valuable learning experiences and share your stories of how setbacks have helped you grow.

This approach helps your teen view mistakes as learning opportunities instead of failures. When they express interest in something new, actively nurture their curiosity by offering resources like books and videos or connecting them with local clubs and groups with similar interests.

Setting Broad Future Goals

Setting broad, adaptable goals can guide your teen toward a positive outlook on their future. Begin by discussing their strengths and interests to identify what excites them. For autistic teens, these discussions help create a sense of purpose, which is critical as they transition to adulthood. However, it is important to stress that goals can—and often do—change over time. Normalizing this flexibility prevents your teen from feeling pressured to follow a rigid path.

You can use real-life examples of people who shifted careers or pursued different passions later in life to illustrate the benefits of being open to change. This understanding allows them to focus on building skills and experiences rather than feeling constrained by a single path.

Building Resilience Through Challenges

Building resilience plays a crucial role in preparing your teen for the future. Resilient teens can better handle setbacks and adjust to new situations. To motivate your teen, share personal stories of overcoming challenges or highlight public figures who thrived despite adversity. Some teens might find inspiration in stories of business leaders or athletes who faced obstacles early on but achieved success through persistence.

You can build resilience by guiding your teen through problem-solving strategies. Show them how to break challenges into smaller, manageable steps, discuss potential solutions, weigh the pros and cons, and choose a course of action. This structured approach strengthens their resilience and sharpens their critical thinking skills.

Building resilience and flexibility in your teen is a long-term process. Still, with consistent encouragement and support, they can face an unpredictable future with greater confidence and optimism. By celebrating small victories and emphasizing growth over perfection, you can help your teen embrace change and view challenges as opportunities for growth.

Key Takeaways

- Celebrating minor victories fosters a sense of achievement and motivation through positive reinforcement.

- Small achievements like initiating conversations deserve recognition as they symbolize growth.

- Involving peers and family in celebrations strengthens community bonds and increases self-esteem.

- Positive reinforcement like targeted praise or small rewards encourages teens to repeat positive behaviors.

- Gradually balancing tangible rewards with verbal praise promotes intrinsic motivation.

- When your teen helps set goals, they take ownership and actively engage in their learning journey.

- Mentorship, community programs, and online courses offer diverse opportunities for skill enhancement.

- Encouraging curiosity and self-reflection promotes growth and emotional resilience.

- Building resilience through problem-solving and storytelling prepares teens for real-world challenges.

Celebrating small wins and using positive reinforcement builds a strong foundation of confidence, resilience, and motivation for autistic teens. Recognizing their achievements and supporting lifelong learning empowers them to embrace challenges, pursue new goals, and develop the skills needed for long-term success and independence.

Conclusion

As we come to the end of this book, it is essential to reflect on the journey we have taken together. We have traveled through an exploration of the unique challenges that autistic teenagers face and touched upon the very essence of fostering independence and self-advocacy. Each chapter has been crafted with care to equip you with the tools and insights necessary for supporting your teen as they transition into adulthood. The roadmap in these pages aims to be a guiding light, a companion in your pursuit of empowerment and hope for the future.

Embarking on a significant journey can be daunting, but remember, you are not alone. Countless parents, educators, and advocates share the same path, united by a common goal: to ensure that every autistic teen can thrive as an adult. These shared adventures create a firm foundation of resilience, connecting us through stories and strategies that unite us. Your supportive community understands and walks with you on this journey.

The nuances of autism can sometimes make the road to independence feel overwhelming. But imagine standing at the threshold of your child's future, feeling empowered and hopeful because you have equipped yourself with the proper support and guidance. With every new skill mastered, from essential daily living tasks to nurturing social connections, you are paving the way for a brighter tomorrow.

Visualize each small success as a stepping stone, contributing to building a more confident and independent young adult. There will undoubtedly be challenges, but these moments of growth are invaluable. Encouraging self-advocacy and independence is not just about preparing your teen for the future; it is about celebrating who they are now and recognizing their potential to achieve great things.

One of the core themes reiterated throughout this book is the necessity of a robust support system. Think of yourself as part of an intricate web, where each thread represents family, friends, educators, and community resources. These threads create a net strong enough to support your teen's aspirations and dreams. By connecting with advocacy groups, engaging with extended family, and collaborating with educators, you harness the collective power of the community.

This sense of community provides more than tangible support; it also fosters a spirit of inclusivity and belonging. When your teen sees the commitment of those around them, they gain confidence knowing they are not navigating these transitions alone. They feel the strength from such unified support and are motivated to push further toward their goals.

Lifelong learning and adaptability play an essential role. The path to adulthood follows a non-linear route, filled with highs, lows, achievements, and challenges. Embracing the notion that life is an ongoing educational experience can transform how we approach changes and challenges. This mindset helps autistic teens build resilience and explore possibilities they once thought were out of reach.

Maintain an open mind as you assess your teen's future. While we naturally have hopes and dreams for our children, allowing space for flexibility and growth cultivates an environment where they can define their paths. This adaptability ensures that no challenge is impossible, and each new experience becomes a valuable lesson, ultimately enriching their lives and fortifying their resolve. Embracing adaptability equips you with the tools to navigate the journey ahead.

Furthermore, fostering a love for learning cannot be overstated. Curiosity and the willingness to learn propel us forward, making us adaptable to life's ever-changing landscape. Instilling this value in our teens means they consider challenges as development possibilities rather than obstacles to progress. This love for learning opens up opportunities for your teen, making their future brighter and more promising.

To the educators reading this book, your role is pivotal. You create a seamless connection between home and school, offering consistency and support that significantly enhances the lives of these teens. Your dedication and innovative approaches can inspire significant shifts in how these young individuals perceive themselves and their abilities. You are the champions who can turn educational settings into fertile grounds for these teens to flourish.

Finally, thank you for your tireless efforts to the advocacy groups and organizations standing alongside families. You raise awareness, share valuable resources, and support autistic teens by enhancing their quality of life. Your work ensures that families are not left to navigate these transitions alone, spotlighting a clear path toward independence and dignity for all.

As we conclude, let us embrace the collective wisdom shared here and apply it daily. Every strategy, insight, and advice is a building block in constructing a supportive and empowering environment for our teens. Teens often face numerous hurdles as they transition into adulthood. Still, the journey also holds immense potential for joy, growth, and newfound independence.

Celebrate each stage onward, no matter how small, as a meaningful victory. Continue to foster hope, encourage growth, and remain steadfast in your support. The future brims with possibilities, and with courage, commitment, and collaboration, your teen can thrive as an independent, resilient adult. Thank you for being part of this journey and for your unwavering dedication to making a meaningful difference in the lives of autistic teenagers. The road ahead may be long, but together, we can make it a journey filled with promise and possibility.

Author Bio

Magen Ross, a parent of an autistic child, holds a master's degree in forensic psychology. She leverages her experience and expertise in self-awareness and healthy relationship strategies to identify negative patterns and self-esteem issues contributing to dysfunction in parenting, relationships, and personal lives.

Magen hopes to empower men, women, and families with practical strategies and techniques. She helps them understand ingrained behaviors, build healthy relationships, set realistic priorities, and address challenges and traumas that impact their success.

Thank You

Dear Reader,

Thank you for deciding to read this inspiring book. I am passionate about helping teens and adults reach their fullest potential, and creating this book has been immensely rewarding. I hope it inspires you as much as it has inspired me.

As a reader, you may need to realize how vital reviews are for authors and how challenging they can be to obtain. Please take a moment to share your thoughts on Amazon, even if it is just a short response.

You can also use the QR code provided to make it easier!

Your feedback not only helps me but also plays a crucial role in increasing the visibility of this work. Reviews on Amazon can significantly impact the book's ranking and visibility, making it more likely to reach and inspire more readers. Your support also contributes to the publication of future self-help resources.

I am grateful for your time and support. I value and relish your insights. You play an influential part in this journey!

Warmest regards, and happy reading!

Magen

References

Autism in the workforce. (2021, September 14). Technical Assitance Center for Quality Employment. https://tacqe.com/autism-in-the-workforce-factsheet/

Autism spectrum disorder. (n.d.). National Institute of Mental Health. https://www.nimh.nih.gov/health/topics/autism-spectrum-disorders-asd

Autism spectrum disorder in teenagers and adults. (2024, May 16). CDC. https://www.cdc.gov/autism/about/asd-in-teenagers-adults.html

Banda, D. R., & Grimmett, E. (2008, September). Enhancing social and transition behaviors of persons with autism through activity schedules: A review. *Education and Training in Developmental Disabilities, 43*(3), 324-333. https://www.jstor.org/stable/23879794

Benefits of mentoring for young people. (n.d.). Youth.gov. https://youth.gov/youth-topics/mentoring/benefits-mentoring-young-people

Bergland, C. (2013, May 30). *The secret to achieving a big goal is...* Psychology Today. https://www.psychologytoday.com/intl/blog/the-athletes-way/201305/the-secret-to-achieving-a-big-goal-is

Danoff-Burg, S., Rus, H. M., Martir, L. C., & Raymann, R. J. (2020, April). 1203 worth the weight: Weighted blanket improves sleep and increases relaxation. *Sleep, 43*(Supplement 1), A460. https://academic.oup.com/sleep/article/43/Supplement_1/A460/5846888?login=false

Day, R. D. (2010, March 30). Stephen Gavazzi: Strong families, successful students: Helping teenagers reach their full potential. *Journal of Youth and Adolescence, 39,* 704-705. https://link.springer.com/article/10.1007/s10964-010-9525-6

Drogomyretska, K., Fox, R., & Colbert, D. (2020). Brief report: Stress and perceived social support in parents of children with ASD. *Journal of Autism and Developmental Disorders, 50,* 4176-4182. https://link.springer.com/article/10.1007/s10803-020-04455-x

Elias, M. J. (2016, January 14). *How and why intrinsic motivation works.* Edutopia. https://www.edutopia.org/blog/how-and-why-intrinsic-motivation-works-maurice-elias

Graham, M. A. (n.d.). *The top 5 things to know when your child with disabilities turns 18.* Special Needs Alliance. https://www.specialneedsalliance.org/blog/the-top-5-things-to-know-when-your-child-with-disabilities-turns-18/

Harvey, M. W. (2001). *The efficacy of vocational education for students with disabilities concerning post-school employment outcomes: A review of the literature.* Scholarly Communication. https://scholar.lib.vt.edu/ejournals/JITE/v38n3/harvey.html

Holmes, B. (2022, January 21). *The science behind exercise for mental health.* Knowable Magazine. https://www.smithsonianmag.com/science-nature/how-exercise-boosts-the-brain-and-improves-mental-health-180979511/

Hotton, M., & Coles, S. (2016). The effectiveness of social skills training groups for individuals with autism spectrum disorder. *Review Journal of Autism and Developmental Disorders, 3,* 68-81. https://link.springer.com/article/10.1007/s40489-015-0066-5

Hutten, M. (2015). *Teaching self-reflection skills to children and teens on the autism spectrum.* My ASD Child. https://www.myaspergerschild.com/2015/12/teaching-self-reflection-skills-to.html

Kesherim, R. (2024, July 2). *Easing change for children with autism: Tips and strategies*. Supportive Care ABA. https://www.supportivecareaba.com/aba-therapy/easing-change-for-children-with-autism

Kojovic, N., Hadid, L. B., Franchini, M., & Schaer, M. (2019). Sensory processing issues and their association with social difficulties in children with autism spectrum disorders. *Journal of Clinical Medicine*, *8*(10), 1508. https://www.mdpi.com/2077-0383/8/10/1508

Lee, A. M.I. (n.d.). *What is IEP transition planning?* Understood.org. https://www.understood.org/en/articles/iep-transition-planning-preparing-for-young-adulthood

Life skills for autism. (n.d.). Autism Speaks. https://www.autismspeaks.org/life-skills-for-autism

MacMillan, C. (2021, September 16). *Why telehealth for mental health care is working*. Yale Medicine. https://www.yalemedicine.org/news/telehealth-for-mental-health

Mediation. (2017, May 2). US Department of Education. https://sites.ed.gov/idea/regs/b/e/300.506

Parenteau, C. I., Floyd, J., Ankenman, K., Glavin, T., Charalel, J., Lin, E., Ence, W., Kim, Y. S., Bishop, S., & Zheng, S. (2024). Efficacy of Community-Delivered PEERS® for Adolescents: Increases in Social Skills and Decreases in Social Anxiety and Loneliness. *Journal of Autism and Developmental Disorders*. https://link.springer.com/article/10.1007/s10803-024-06433-z

Sarris, M. (2013, July 23). *Autism in the Teen Years: What to Expect, How to Help*. Kennedy Krieger Institute. https://www.kennedykrieger.org/stories/interactive-autism-network-ian/autism_in_teens

Sawisz, B. (2023, May 25). *Harnessing the power of positive reinforcement*. Psychology Today.

https://www.psychologytoday.com/us/blog/nurturing-self-esteem-in-autistic-children/202305/harnessing-the-power-of-positive

Selig, M. (2012, July 18). *The amazing power of "small wins"*. Psychology Today. https://www.psychologytoday.com/sg/blog/changepower/201207/the-amazing-power-of-small-wins

Smith, T. E., Sheridan, S. M., Kim, E. M., Park, S., & Beretvas, S. N. (2020). The effects of family-school partnership interventions on academic and social-emotional functioning: A meta-analysis exploring what works for whom. *Educational Psychology Review, 32*, 511-544. https://link.springer.com/article/10.1007/s10648-019-09509-w

Spotlight on achieving a better life experience (ABLE) accounts. (n.d.). SSA. https://www.ssa.gov/ssi/spotlights/spot-able.html

10 ways extended family can make a difference for individuals with autism. (2023, November 4). Autism Connect. https://www.autismconnect.com/blogs/individuals-with-autism/

Transition-age youth and social security – Age 18 re-determination. (2018, October 1). Disability Rights California. https://www.disabilityrightsca.org/publications/transition-age-youth-and-social-security-age-18-re-determination

Updated clinical report on health care transitions for youth and young adults. (2018, October 22). HealthyChildren.org. https://www.healthychildren.org/English/news/Pages/Health-Care-Transitions-For-Youth-and-Young-Adults.aspx

Wandering prevention. (n.d.). Autism Speaks. https://www.autismspeaks.org/wandering-prevention

Wang, C. (2024, April 29). *Understanding the underpinnings of sensory hypersensitivity in SCN2A-associated autism.* National Institute of

Mental Health. https://www.nimh.nih.gov/news/science-news/2024/understanding-the-underpinnings-of-sensory-hypersensitivity-in-scn2a-associated-autism

Weiss, J., & LeBlanc, J. (2019, October 1). *Strengthening community engagement with vocational training and employment for young adults with autism.* Autism Spectrum News. https://autismspectrumnews.org/strengthening-community-engagement-with-vocational-training-and-employment-for-young-adults-with-autism/

Whiteside, E. (2024, August 22). *The 50/30/20 budget rule explained with examples.* Investopedia. https://www.investopedia.com/ask/answers/022916/what-502030-budget-rule.asp

Made in United States
North Haven, CT
22 August 2025

71974333R00111